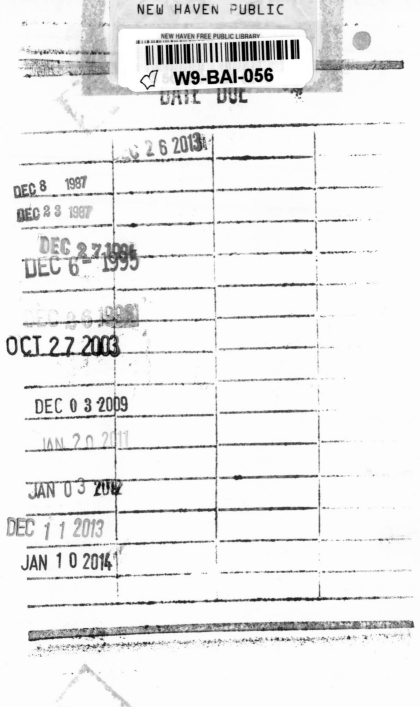

Virginie Fowler

CHRISTMAS CRAFTS & CUSTOMS

AROUND THE WORLD

❖ ❖ ❖

illustrations by the author

Prentice-Hall, Inc./Englewood Cliffs, New Jersey

And a Merry Christmas
to David

Printed in the United States of America   ·J

Prentice-Hall International, Inc., London
Prentice-Hall of Australia, Pty. Ltd., Sydney
Prentice-Hall Canada, Inc., Toronto
Prentice-Hall of India Private Ltd., New Delhi
Prentice-Hall of Japan, Inc., Tokyo
Prentice-Hall of Southeast Asia Pte. Ltd., Singapore
Whitehall Books Limited, Wellington, New Zealand
Editora Prentice-Hall do Brasil LTDA., Rio de Janeiro

10 9 8 7 6 5 4 3

Library of Congress Cataloging in Publication Data
Elbert, Virginie Fowler
    Christmas crafts and customs around the world.
    Summary: Presents traditional customs, crafts, and
recipes from various countries around the world.
    1. Christmas decorations—Juvenile literature.
2. Christmas cookery—Juvenile literature. 3. Christmas—Juvenile literature. [1. Christmas decorations.
2. Christmas cookery. 3. Christmas] I. Title.
TT900.C4E43 1984   394.2'68282   84-9770
ISBN 0-13-133661-4

Contents

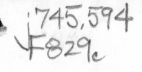

Christmas Around the World 1

England 4
　Mistletoe Ball 5
　Mincemeat-Filled Cookies 8
　Pomander Balls 11
　Hot Mulled Cider 13
　Walnut Shell Cradle 15
　Victorian Fan Decoration 18

France 21
　Santons of Provence 22
　Christmas Paper Crackers 30
　Twelfth Night Cake 32
　Twelfth Night Crowns 35

Germany 40
　Advent Calendar 41
　Tiny Christmas Angel 45
　Square-Top Cornucopia 48
　Honey Spice Cookies 51
　Woolly Sheep 54

Greece 61
Courambiades 62

Holland 65
Dutch "Wooden" Shoe 65
Initial Letter Cookies 69

Italy 72
Nativity Scene Figures 73

Scandinavia 76
Wooden Cutouts for the Tree 77
St. Lucia Buns ("Cats") 79
Wooden Candle-Tree 82
Wheat Wreath 87

Thailand 90
Straw Fish 90

China 97
Proud Peacock 97

The Philippines 102
Christmas Star 103

United States 108
Christmas Card 109
Christmas Stocking 112
Puffed Rice Molasses Balls 116
Ribbon Christmas Ball 117
New England Bread Stuffing 121
Appalachian Braided Wreath 123
South Carolina Orange Sweet Potatoes 126
Ambrosia 128

Central and South America and the Caribbean Islands   130

Piñata Fish   132

Angel of Clay   138

Gourd Noisemaker   141

Benne Balls   143

Before You Begin   146

Helpful Hints   146

Where to Buy Supplies   146

Baking and Cooking   148

Block Printing with Styrofoam   152

Clay   154

Gluing and Cementing   156

Grid Method of Enlarging and
    Reducing Designs   157

Lead-Pencil Transfer Paper   158

Paper, Cutting and Gluing   159

Painting   162

Papier-Mâché   164

Salt Dough   165

Sewing Fabric   166

Working with Wood   169

Christmas
Around the World

❖ ❖ ❖

Christmas around the world is a thirty-day festival. All the countries of Europe and North and South America celebrate in their special ways from Advent and December 6, Saint Nicholas Day, to January 6, which is Epiphany, also known as Twelfth Night or Three Kings' Day. In some countries the gift-giving day is December 6, in others it is Christmas Eve or Christmas Day, and in still others it is January 6. There are in all the countries of Europe small differences in local customs, some from pagan days, that have been blended into the traditions of Christmastime.

Advent begins four Sundays before Christmas Day to celebrate the coming of Christ. Epiphany, January 6, is when the Three Magi or Kings first saw the Christ Child in Bethlehem. January 6 is also known as Twelfth Night, since it is twelve days after the birth of Christ on December 25, and it had taken the Magi twelve days to reach Bethlehem. In some countries the day is called Three Kings' Day.

In much of Africa and Asia, Christianity is not the religion of the local people, so Christmas is not celebrated. But there are many small areas in these continents that have been settled at one time or another by European colonists or by missionaries, or where United States troops have been stationed, and there Christmas customs are followed. Where there has been a succession of colonists—French, Spanish, and English in the Caribbean Islands—Christmas becomes a joyous, mixed-up celebration as each ethnic group helps the other to celebrate *their* day!

In warm countries, the northern snow-and-cold-weather celebration has been adapted to the climate. In Australia, for example, December 25 is midsummer, so while everyone still has a traditional English dinner including mince pie, the afternoon is spent swimming in the ocean or pool.

India has a mixture of British and Indian celebrations because the Hindu Harvest Festival runs into the British Christmas season, while the Tamil Christians hold their own religious services and carol sings.

In Thailand where Buddhism is the country's religion, American troops were stationed and the French had established church schools, so there is a certain amount of Western influence. Some department stores are decorated, gifts are exchanged, and potted Norfolk Island pines (that are not pine trees at all) are trimmed with strips of cotton batting laid on their branches to simulate snow.

Japan, too, has a "department store" Christmas, and along with China and India the Japanese make Christmas tree ornaments that are shipped to the United States.

Africa and the Middle East where Europeans have settled have Christmas-season celebrations that reflect the home countries, while the Christian Coptic Church follows ancient customs. Our Christmas had its beginnings in Bethlehem, and there the religious mood is strong with a solemn Midnight Mass on Christmas Eve.

South American celebrations are completely Spanish, except for Portuguese Brazil, with only here and there some leftover tribal customs which have blended into the Christian celebration. In many of these countries and in Puerto Rico, Christmas Eve and Christmas Day are religious days, with Midnight Mass followed by a large Christmas feast. The Twelve Days of Christmas becomes a time of feasting and partying, ending on Three Kings' Day when the camels of the Magi bring presents to the children.

The United States, having been settled by many nationalities, has a mixture of customs that vary from place to place, depending on the background of the early colonists. From the Dutch in New York to the Puritan English in New England and the Royalist English in the south, the Greeks in Florida, Germans in Pennsylvania, French in Louisiana, Scandinavians in Minnesota, and Spanish in California, with many others in between, we have a wonderful mixture of the many ways to celebrate a joyful season.

In this book you'll find more details of local customs, traditional crafts to make, and local Christmas-season foods to make and eat, so you can either celebrate in one country's style, or go international and make your own glorious mix of many countries.

England

✤ ✤ ✤

Some Christmas customs are very ancient: the mistletoe of the Druids (whose religion was practiced as early as 200 B.C.) was known as the all-healer, and was gathered in midwinter to ward off evil spirits; in pagan times a Yule log was burned through the dark days of December to bring good luck and the ashes were scattered around the fruit trees for a good harvest. Yule is a Scandinavian and northern European word that now refers to the Christmas season.

At Glastonbury Abbey, southwest of London, legend has it that the original wattle church was built by Joseph of Arimathea around 66 A.D., and the thorn staff that he stuck in the ground took root and bloomed each year at Christmastime. And there is still a Glastonbury thornbush that blooms each year at Christmastime.

As far back as the fourteenth century, groups of men called Mummers roamed the streets of their villages; dressed in disguises, they had the right to enter any house to dance and sing, to give brief plays, and generally entertain during the Christmas season, bringing good luck to the house. All over England the Mummers' plays took place, and each county had different customs that had developed over the centuries, all involved in the celebration of the harvest and designed to ensure the health of the household, the farm animals, trees and fields. The plays and merrymaking were the release from the hard work of fields and barns and a breathing space before the next year's work began.

These early customs slowly changed, and in the fifteenth century it became popular to elect a Lord of Misrule with a whole court of helpers for the Christmas ceremonies at court and the homes of the nobility, as well as at the colleges. The plays became more elaborate as did the feasting, games, and pranks.

At the court of Henry the Eighth in the sixteenth century, the Christmas season up through Twelfth Night was a joyous time. Elaborate dramatic productions, known as masques, and balls were held at the palace in Greenwich, down the River Thames from London. There is a scene in Shakespeare's *Henry VIII* of a simple masque with the king disguised as a shepherd surprising Cardinal Wolsey at a banquet. His daughter, Queen Elizabeth I, continued the customs of Christmastime, and Shakespeare's play *Twelfth Night* was performed for her on January 6, 1601.

Then suddenly, all the joyous times were stopped when Oliver Cromwell, after several years of civil war, became head of state in 1653, and his strict Puritan beliefs became law. After his death a few years later, it was a long time before there was any return to a Christmas of gift giving and feasting and celebrating the old customs.

In the middle of the nineteenth century under Queen Victoria, Christmas became a celebration of children's joys; of gifts, decorated trees, Santa Claus (or Klaus), and family feasts. Boxing Day (the day after Christmas) became a holiday, as the boxes of servants and tradespeople were filled with gifts and money. And this is how Christmas is still celebrated in England.

MISTLETOE BALL

All sorts of evergreens are gathered together in a loose ball, with a sprig or more of mistletoe dangling from the bottom. Each of the greens has an ancient meaning and the custom of hanging balls of greens at Christmastime goes back to the fifteenth century, as a promise of green to come.

Evergreen twigs and branches, representing the spring to come, were cut in the winter when all the other trees had lost their leaves. Mistletoe was the only plant which bore fruit in the winter and so it was considered magical. It was also part of the Druids' religion, practiced long before Christianity came to England, and so was often forbidden in early churches. The holly was a man's plant, and ivy, a woman's plant; they were both part of the ball, as both stayed green in the wintertime. Small red apples (crab apples or lady apples) and bows of bright ribbon were added for decoration.

And like all Christmas decorations the ball was taken down after Twelfth Night and often burned to ensure good luck. But, quite the contrary in some sections of the country, pieces were kept until the next Christmas, to ensure good luck!

Materials and Tools
twigs of spruce, hemlock, pine, cedar, laurel, holly leaves and
    berries, mistletoe, and lengths of ivy (some or all of these)
2 wire coat hangers
fine wire or braided picture wire, 20 feet
satin ribbon, ¼ inch wide, 5 yards (for 20 bows), red
small red apples (optional)
pomander ball (optional), see page 11
ruler
wire clipper
pliers
scissors

Note: Christmas greens in small pieces can often be picked up for free at the lots where trees and greens are sold. Ask the person in charge of the lot for permission to take the pieces.

Directions

1. Slowly turn the hook of one hanger until it is at right angles to the hanger.

2. Measure 15 inches from each side of the hook on both hangers, and cut at that point with the wire clippers.

3. Curve the two sides of the wire around until a rough circle is formed. (You'll never be able to smooth out completely the rounded points on each side.) With the pliers twist together 1 inch of the wire ends. Repeat with the other hanger.

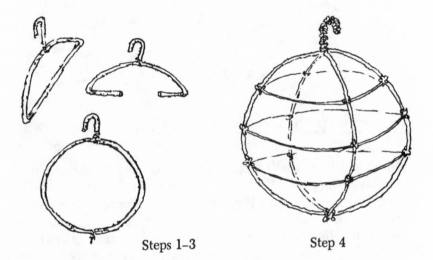

Steps 1–3   Step 4

4. Slip one circle inside the other, so the circles are at right angles to each other and the hooks face in the same direction. Bind the hooks together with fine wire. Fasten lengths of fine wire horizontally between the four heavy wires to act as supports for the greens. You can unbraid the picture wire into separate strands, using two of the strands twisted together.

5. Now you're on your own. With fine wire, fasten your choice of greens to the heavy-wire circles and the fine-wire crosspieces, forming a ball of greenery. Drape ivy around the outside, either horizontally or vertically. You can hang small apples here

and there, attaching them to the heavy wires. Add the mistletoe at the bottom where all can see it for holiday kissing greetings.

6. Make small bows of red ribbon and attach them to the greens with fine wire. Add ribbon loops around the top of the ball, attaching them to the wire hook.

7. Hang the green ball from a center chandelier, or suspend from the ceiling or a doorway.

Variation: You can hang a pomander ball (see page 11 for directions) below the mistletoe, or in place of the mistletoe.

MINCEMEAT-FILLED COOKIES

Mincemeat pies, small or large, have been a traditional Christmas sweet since the Middle Ages. All sorts of customs and beliefs have grown up around the making and serving of the pies. In Medieval days they were boat-shaped or rectangular and represented the Holy Cradle; the filling with its eastern spices represented the gifts of the Magi. These shapes were easy to form and bake on the flat stone floors of the ovens. In the 1500s in England it was believed that eating a piece of mincemeat pie on each of the Twelve Days of Christmas would bring good luck for the next twelve months. For this reason large pies were set out on a table for visitors to help themselves. The Puritan ruler Cromwell, when he came to power in 1653, forbade the making and serving of rectangular mince pies because they were part of the Christmas holiday celebration, and so the housewives baked their pies in circular metal pans.

In Medieval days these pies were eaten as a meal, not just a dessert. The hearty filling was made of minced meat and suet chopped fine, with raisins, spices, and sugar added. The mixture was cooked and put in a large glazed clay crock to ripen. The sugar and spices preserved the meat in those days of no refrigeration and gave the filling a tasty flavor. The use of raisins and spices may mean that this recipe was brought back from the Middle East by the Crusaders.

In Victorian days, when Mother was making mincemeat pies for Christmas dinner, she would break off some of the pie crust dough and scoop some mincemeat from the crock so the children could make mincemeat turnovers (rounds of dough folded over the mincemeat and sealed along the edge). After the coal stove's oven had become hot enough, the pies went in as well as the baking sheet filled with turnovers. When the turnovers were taken out of the oven, the children hung around the cooling rack in the pantry waiting for the moment when they could be picked up and eaten without burning their fingers and tongues.

Here is a recipe using a simple sugar cookie dough for round cookies. The mincemeat filling is placed between two cookies before baking. The mincemeat (already prepared) is bought in a jar.

Read the section on Baking in the last chapter before beginning the recipe.

CAUTION: Never use sharp kitchen equipment or the stove or oven without asking a responsible adult to help you.

Ingredients
This will make about 18 covered cookies.

3 tablespoons butter, plus butter for baking sheet
   (or margarine)
4½ tablespoons sugar
½ teaspoon vanilla
1 egg
⅞ cup flour
pinch of salt
¾ teaspoon baking powder
1½ tablespoons milk
1 cup mincemeat
2½-inch round cookie cutter, plain or fluted edge

Directions

1. Butter a baking sheet and set aside.

2. Sift flour, baking powder, and salt together into a small bowl.

3. In a larger bowl cream butter until smooth, add sugar and mix well, then add vanilla and mix again.

4. Beat egg in a small bowl, and add half the egg to the butter and sugar mixture. The rest of the egg, mixed with ½ teaspoon of water, will be brushed on the top of the cookies before baking.

5. Now combine the flour with the mixture of butter, sugar, and egg, alternating with the milk. If dough is too stiff and floury, add a little more milk, a teaspoon at a time, mixing it in before adding any more.

6. Roll out the dough ⅛ inch thick between two floured sheets of wax paper. Cut out cookies with cookie cutter. Place half the cookies on the buttered baking sheet, lining them up evenly with an inch between each cookie. Set other cookies to one side on the pastry board. Gather up the scraps, roll out the dough again, and cut out more cookies. Repeat until all dough is used up.

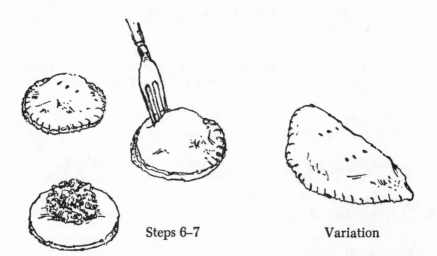

Steps 6–7   Variation

7. Measure out the mincemeat into a cup. Place a measuring teaspoon of mincemeat in the center of each cookie on the baking sheet. Moisten the cookie edges with water or milk. Cover with

the second cookie and press edges together with index finger, then go around the edges with the tines of a table fork to seal and decorate the edges. Stab the center of each cookie with the pointed ends of the tines to let out steam. Brush tops of the cookies with the rest of the egg, using a pastry brush, so they will turn a golden brown in baking.

8. Put baking sheet in the middle of a preheated 400° oven for 15 minutes. Take out, remove cookies from sheet with a wide cake turner, and place on a cooling rack.

Variation: Using a larger cookie cutter (3½ to 4 inches) and more filling, you can fold the circle in half over the filling for turnovers.

POMANDER BALLS

Words, translated and mispronounced over the centuries from country to country, lose their original spelling and meaning. "Pome" refers to an apple (or other round fruit) or a ball; "ander" refers to amber, a yellow-to-orange fossil resin. So pomander becomes a ball of amber, or an orange ball.

Pomander balls with their fragrance of orange and cloves celebrate the southern world of wintertime oranges and the spices that were brought to Bethlehem by the Magi. Hung from chandeliers, they promised a return of the sun so sorely missed in the cold, gray England of December.

They were put into chests full of clothes and were carried to the theaters in Elizabethan days, as their clean, spicy odor overcame the smells of the crowded playhouses.

You can make several pomander balls to hang in rooms, closets, and on the tree, or add one to the mistletoe ball (see page 5). Make extra balls to give to friends.

Materials and Tools
orange, soft-skinned, medium size
cloves, approximately one 1¾-ounce box
satin ribbon, ½ inch wide, color of your choice
thin nail or small ¹⁄₁₆-inch-wide skewer
thin string
scissors

Directions
1. Make a small hole in the skin of the orange with the thin nail or skewer. Stick a clove in the hole. Repeat this process all over the orange, until the surface is well-covered, yet there is enough skin showing to separate the cloves. Number of cloves used depends on the size of the orange.

Step 1

2. Temporarily tie string around the orange, bottom to top on four sides with a loop at the top. Hang the pomander ball in a cool dry place until the surface begins to dry and the orange has started to shrink a bit.

3. Remove the string and add a bright-colored ribbon, tying it in the same way as the string, with a loop at the top, as long as is needed to hang up the pomander ball. The length of the ribbon depends on the size of the orange and the length of the hanging loop.

HOT MULLED CIDER

Serving hot mulled cider to caroling groups on the cold nights of Christmastime is an old tradition in England and some other European countries. The group singing of carols is a custom going back to pagan days, with many changes of meaning and types of songs. In the Middle Ages a ring dance with songs was called a carol, and it was a joyous pastime all through the year as groups linked hands, singing as they danced in a circle. Gradually the dancing and singing was forbidden by the church.

In the thirteenth century, Saint Francis of Assisi turned the songs into sacred ones, and as this new form traveled across Europe to England, the songs centered on Christmas. Minstrels at medieval feasts during the Twelve Days of Christmas sang these carols and others of their own writing. Minstrel-sung carols were part of the Christmastime feasts at the Court of King Arthur. Most of the old carols have disappeared from popular singing, and those we know today were written in the eighteenth and nineteenth centuries.

From the eighteenth century on, carolers would stop in front of each house to sing a Christmas carol and would be invited inside by their neighbors to warm up with a pewter mug of hot, mulled cider. Sometimes a spoonful of baked apple, called lamb's wool, was added to the cider. Other times the hot cider was carried out to the group as they were singing.

You can make this recipe for the family as they trim the tree, serving the hot cider in china mugs.

Before you begin, read the Do's and Don'ts under Baking in the last chapter.

CAUTION: Never use sharp kitchen equipment or the stove or oven without asking a responsible adult to help you.

Ingredients
> apple cider
> cinnamon sticks, 2–3 inches long
> whole cloves
> sugar

Directions

1. Measure out the amount of cider you will need by filling and refilling a mug, the amount depending on how many people you are serving. Pour cider into a saucepan large enough to hold the quantity you are making.

2. Allow one stick of cinnamon, three cloves, and one teaspoon of sugar for each mug. Add spices and sugar to the cider, and bring to a boil.

3. Ladle the hot cider into the mugs, being sure that a stick of cinnamon is added to each mug.

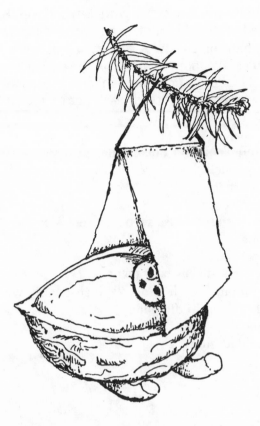

WALNUT SHELL CRADLE

In Victorian times as the holiday season approached, large baskets of walnuts from France, Spain, or Italy, and bunches of Malaga raisins dried on their stems appeared in English stores. The combination of nuts and raisins had been a favorite end-of-dinner combination from medieval days, or later on as a special after-school snack. Nuts were used in the Christmas fruitcakes, mincemeat, and cookies which the whole family joined in making; the children helped shell walnuts and almonds and cut up dried and candied fruits.

Walnut shells were carefully cracked so the two halves remained unbroken and the meats could be taken out whole. The unbroken shells were set aside to be made into Christmas decorations. Two halves could be glued together with a string loop between them, then covered with gold paint to be hung on the tree or used in wreaths or balls of greens. A half shell was made into a cradle with rockers and canopy to hang on the tree or to use as a doll-house toy. The decorations were made after school or on Saturdays and, as everyone worked, each person took a turn reading aloud from a favorite book.

Materials and Tools (for one cradle)
half a walnut shell
thin wire, 11 inches
lightweight cardboard
basket reed or round balsa wood dowel, ⅛ × 5 inches
masking tape
absorbent cotton
fabric, 1½ × 2½ inches, any color
grosgrain ribbon, ¾ inch wide, 2½ inches long, white
wood bead, ⅜ inch in diameter
contact cement
white household glue
pencil
ruler
scissors
craft knife
felt-tipped pen, black

Step 1

Directions
   1. Cut 5 inches of thin wire in half with the scissors. Curve each 2½-inch piece around the bottom of the half walnut shell, one piece almost at the pointed "front," the other almost at the broad "back." Curve them up at each end but away from the shell. Cut off any extra wire. Lay each piece on the cardboard, and trace along the curve with a pencil, marking them for front or back.

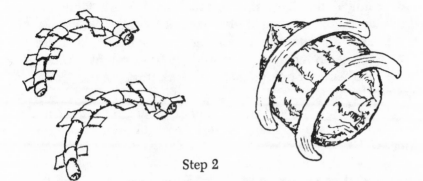

Step 2

2. Before straightening out the wires, mark the front one with a small smudge of the felt-tipped pen. Straighten out the two wires, and use them to cut the right lengths of reed or dowel. Soak the two pieces in water for at least three hours or until soft enough to be bent into shallow curves. Slowly bend the reed or dowel pieces so the inner edge fits the two curves drawn on the cardboard, front and back lengths. Tape into place until dry. These are the two rockers for the cradle. Attach to bottom of shell with contact cement.

3. Fill the shell with absorbent cotton, mounding it up to a slight curve at the top. Remove in one piece and lightly wrap the piece of fabric around it. Glue the 1½-inch edges together with white glue and let dry.

4. Put a few drops of white glue in the bottom of the shell and along the sides and press the fabric-covered cotton in place, tucking in all the edges, seam against the bottom of the shell.

 Step 5

5. With the felt-tipped pen add a face to the wooden bead: two dots for eyes and one for the mouth, plus a few wisps of hair. Glue the bead with contact cement, face side up, to the upper end of the fabric covered cotton, head against the edge of the shell.

6. Fold the ribbon in half across the ¾-inch width. Glue ends to the outer rim of each side at the broad end of the shell, using contact cement. Back portion may hang free (see drawing). Let dry.

7. Bend the 6 inches of wire so there is a straight ¾-inch section in the center. Slip under the ribbon canopy so this section is against the ribbon fold. Bring ends of the wire together above the canopy and twist to hold. Use this loop to hang the cradle on the tree. Make several cradles for your tree, and others to give to friends.

Variation: If you are making the cradle as a toy, then double the amount of grosgrain ribbon. Cut it in half and place the two lengths of ribbon together. Crease them at the halfway mark, then spread glue on the two matching sides. Before pressing together, place a ¾-inch length of wire at the crease. Then follow the rest of the directions in Step 6.

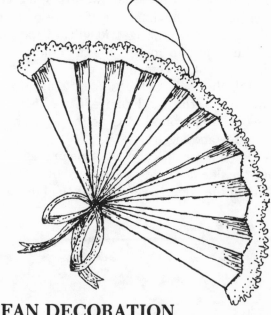

VICTORIAN FAN DECORATION

A decorated Christmas tree was new in Victorian England, brought from Germany by Queen Victoria's husband Albert. Families set about trimming their trees with handcrafted decorations: small paper baskets filled with sweets, cornucopias copied from German models, tiny lace-trimmed paper fans, red apples, pomander balls to sweetly scent the air, and strings of looped paper chains. Added to the homecrafted decorations were fragile imported Christmas tree balls of thin, bright-colored glass, wax angels, and a tinsel star at the top of the tree.

The paper fans were fussily pretty, made of folded gold or silver paper, or shiny colored paper, edged with lace either white or dyed, then decorated with a narrow ribbon bow. These were hung here and there on the large tree. You may do the same, or trim a small tree with only fans in one or several colors.

Materials and Tools
gift-wrap paper, gold or silver, or shiny colored paper
edging lace, 1 inch wide (or lace seam binding, 3-yard
    package)
ribbon, velvet or satin, ¼ inch wide, any color
liquid starch
white household glue
2 paper clips
button and carpet thread, black
pencil
ruler
scissors
flat watercolor brush, ¾ inch wide
small container for mixing glue

Directions
1. For each fan cut two pieces of paper—4 × 10 inches; a 10-inch length of edging lace; a 14-inch length of ribbon; 5 inches of black button and carpet thread for hanging fan on the tree.

2. Dip lace in liquid starch, smooth out, and hang up to dry.

3. When lace is dry, brush on a ¼-inch-wide line of glue along one 10-inch edge of paper, *on the wrong side.* Lay the bottom, straight edge of the lace along the glued edge, pressing it flat. Let dry.

4. Brush slightly thinned glue over both wrong sides of the two pieces of paper and press them together, smoothing carefully. Put a book on top until glue is dry.

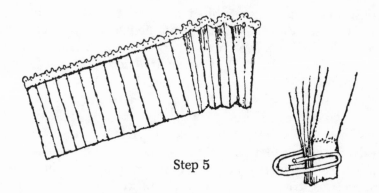

Step 5

5. Measure, rule pencil lines, and fold paper in ½-inch-wide accordion pleats. Brush a ⅜-inch line of glue along the edge opposite the lace. Press the pleats together at this point and hold with a paper clip until dry.

6. Open up the fan as wide as possible, tucking in a small triangle at the bottom of the two side pleats. Hold each triangle in place with glue, clamping each side with a paper clip until dry.

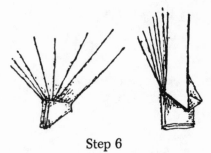

Step 6

7. Tie a bow with the 14 inches of ribbon and glue to the bottom of the fan.

8. At the center of the fan, glue a loop made from the 5-inch length of button and carpet thread.

France

✤ ✤ ✤

At the beginning of Advent in the early part of December, the large Santon Fair opens in the city of Marseilles in the south of France on the Mediterranean Sea, and here the clay crèche figures called *santons* have been sold since the seventeenth century.

In other parts of France, starting on Christmas Eve, it is an ancient custom to keep a Yule Log burning all through the twelve days of Christmas, until Twelfth Night. The fire is smothered each night so the log will last the full time. The farmers sprinkle the ashes around the base of their fruit trees for a good harvest. On Christmas Eve, *Bonhomme Noël* (Christmas Man, or Father Christmas) leaves presents on the hearth for the children. A solemn Christmas Eve Mass is celebrated at church, followed by the ceremonial supper called *réveillon* (which refers to being awake). At this supper and at the main Christmas Day meal many delicacies are served, but also there are certain traditional dishes; a black or white pudding made with sausages, a goose or turkey stuffed with chestnuts, and then whatever else fills out the two meals.

Twelfth Night is a final night of celebration and merriment with the Twelfth Night Cake as the centerpiece. This party is a survival of the pagan feast, Basilinda. The cake takes many forms, depending on the part of France where it is made. But it always contains a hidden bean or a small silver coin. Gold paper crowns are given to the one who finds the bean or coin and to the partner he or she picks. This king and queen rule over the rest of the evening, and sometimes give the next week's party.

SANTONS OF PROVENCE

The tradition of the *Santons de Provence* (Little Saints of Provence) probably can be traced back to St. Francis's first live crèche scene in central Italy in the early part of the thirteenth century. Later on in France in the seventeenth century, actors staged *tableaux vivants* (living pictures) of the scene in the Bethlehem stable as part of the Christmas celebration in the castles of noble families. The titled people were so enchanted by these scenes that they commissioned local potters to make small figures dressed in local costumes that could be set up permanently in their homes. These skills have been handed down through generations of craft families, known as *santonniers*. Through the years new figures were added to the crèche scene, to represent local farmers and tradespeople. But even today, the figures still reflect the life of seventeenth-century Provence, even though some may be newly designed.

The small figures, anywhere from 5 to 12 inches high, are made of clay cast in molds that are part of a family's heritage. The clothes are sometimes painted on and covered with a clear glaze; in other types, the unglazed clay figures are dressed in fabric clothes with the tools or produce of their trade as part of the figure. Each santon-maker family has its own style, and all types are sold at the fair.

People come from all over to the fair to buy the figures for their home crèches, adding to their scenes year after year. Others buy in large quantities to sell in the local shops of Provence and other parts of France, or to ship them out of the country.

Materials and Tools
clay, either oven-baked or air-dried (sold in 2- to
    5-pound boxes)
plastic wrap
thin nail, 1½ inches long
acrylic polymer gloss medium
acrylic paints, white, red, black
tissue paper
fabric, see Step 14 for types and amount
sewing thread to match fabric colors
narrow ribbon or cord, black
round plastic pill bottle with cover, 1½ × 3 inches
bird gravel or sand for pill bottle
white household glue
pencil
ruler
scissors
craft knife
skewer, ¹⁄₁₆ inch in diameter
tools for working with clay
pins
needle
flat nylon brush, ¾ inch wide
round nylon brush, #2
pliers

Directions

1. First, before buying or working with clay, read the section on Clay in the last chapter.

2. Except for the face, hands, and feet, the clay body will be covered with fabric clothes, so the body can be made simply from cylinders of clay. Roll cylinders of clay on a sheet of plastic wrap laid on a flat surface, using the palms of your hands. You can easily form the arms, legs, body, and head of the farmer's wife in this way. Form two arms ⅝ × 4 inches, two legs ¾ × 6 inches, body 1¾ × 2¼ inches, and the head ¾ × 1 inch.

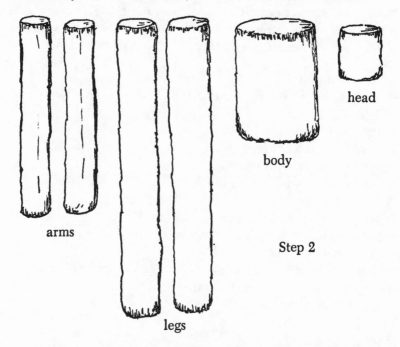

arms

legs

body

head

Step 2

3. Next, a little trimming of the clay will be needed to fit all the pieces together. With the knife, make a ½-inch vertical cut at one end of each arm roll, on the side facing the body. This flat area will be joined to the top of the body cylinder. At the other end of each arm taper 1 inch of the cylinder down to ⅜ inch in diameter to form the lower arm and wrist. Add a flat oval piece of clay at the end for a hand. Bend arms at right angles at the middle of the cylinder, making sure the upper vertical cut will face the body, so the arms will be folded across the body at the waist.

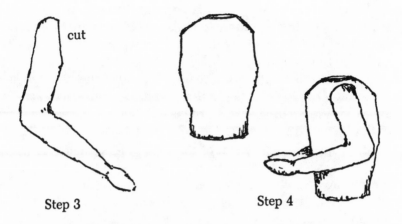

cut

Step 3   Step 4

4. Taper the body cylinder to 1¼ inches at the lower end. At the upper end, curve the top downward to form a sloping shoulder line. Slice away a little clay to form the front and back of the body and smooth into an oval shape. Flatten an area at the top of each narrow side to match the vertical cuts on the upper arms, then attach arms to this area.

5. The finished figure will be seated on the gravel-filled pill bottle and will be held in place with a thin nail that will be attached both to the body and the pill bottle. With the nail, make a 1-inch-deep hole in the middle of the lower part of the cylinder, then remove nail.

6. Make a ½-inch vertical cut at one end of each leg roll, as you did for the arms. Taper the lower 1 inch of the other end of

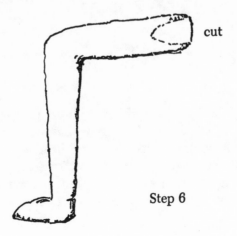

cut

Step 6

the leg cylinders to ½ inch in diameter at the very end. Bend legs at right angles in the middle to make a seated figure; the vertical cut area faces the body. Add a small oval roll of clay at right angles to the bottom of each leg for shoes.

7. With one hand, hold the body on top of the small pill bottle. Attach the top of a leg to the lower side of the body, cutting away a flat matching area on the body. Repeat on the other side of the body with the other leg. The bent knees face forward.

8. Adjust the placement of the legs, pulling them downward a bit if too short, or lifting them up if too long. You may have to flatten the bottom of the upper legs so the *santon* sits solidly on the plastic bottle top. Shoes should fit squarely on the flat working surface with space between them. Allow space between the hands and legs, and body and arms, so the fabric clothes can be added. Make a pencil mark on the cover of the plastic pill bottle to match the nail hole in the bottom of the body.

9. Form the head roll into an egg shape, pointed end at bottom, and attach it to the body with a small narrow roll of clay for the neck. Prick out the features with a small pointed skewer or nail, adding bits of clay for nose, eyebrows, and perhaps the chin area.

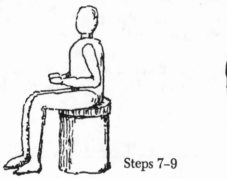

Steps 7–9   Step 9

10. Push the skewer into the body here and there so the clay will dry evenly. Let figure dry very well before baking if you are using oven-baked clay. Legs, arms and head will dry before the body. Air-dried clay should also be well dried.

11. Bake the clay figure if oven-baked, following directions in the last chapter. When cool, proceed to the next step, as the final

finishing of air-dried and oven-baked clay is the same, depending on the color of the clay.

12. If the clay is gray you will have to add a light-colored surface before painting with acrylic polymer gloss medium, as the medium will darken the clay color too much. Mix a little of the red with the white acrylic paint, thinning it with the gloss medium. Paint all surfaces with this mixture using the flat brush, and let dry. When dry, add a second coat and let dry. Paint eyebrows and eyes with black paint and lips with red, using the #2 brush; also add high shoes by covering the foot and ankles with black paint. Let dry. Cover all surfaces with a coat of acrylic polymer gloss medium. Let dry, and add a second coat. Let dry well before dressing the figure.

13. If the clay is terracotta color or pale tan, cover all surfaces with a coat of acrylic polymer gloss medium using the flat brush. Let dry, then cover with a second coat. This is necessary, as oven-baked and air-dried clays are not as strong as kiln-fired clays; the acrylic covering strengthens the surface and keeps the clay from chipping. Often the terracotta *santons* do not have colored features, but if you want to add them, then paint in eyebrows, eyes, lips, plus the shoes after the first coat of the medium. Then cover with the second coat.

14. If the clay is white, follow the directions in Step 12.

15. The *santon* is dressed as a farm woman with her full skirt, blouse, shawl, apron, and cap fitted on her. There can be no exact pattern, as each *santon* will vary in size. Here are suggestions for fabrics: striped or small-patterned material for the skirt, thin white fabric for blouse and cap, black fabric for shawl and apron. If you are buying fabric, the minimum amount you can buy is ¼ yard which is 9 inches. If your mother has a piece box, then go through it and pick fabrics that can be used, but ask permission first.

16. For the skirt pattern, cut a piece of tissue paper 8 × 12 inches and try it around the figure, gathering it on the 12-inch length around the waist to make a full skirt. The 8-inch depth, less a ½-inch hem, should just clear the foot part of the shoes. Make changes in length or width if needed, then use the tissue paper as a pattern, pinning it to the fabric and then cutting out the skirt. Turn up the hem on the wrong side and sew in place.

Add two lines of gathering stitches at the top. On the wrong side, seam the back with a ¼-inch strengthened seam. Set aside. (See Sewing in last chapter for description of stitches.)

17. For the blouse, fold a 10 × 8-inch piece of tissue paper in half on the 8-inch measurement to form a folded piece 10 × 4 inches. In the center of the fold, cut a ½-inch wide by ¼-inch-deep half-circle, and a 1-inch slit from the center of one side of the half-circle, so the blouse pattern can be slipped over the head. Cut very wide sleeves, long enough to reach to the wrists, and cut the body a little full so it will blouse a bit. Allow for ¼-inch seams under the sleeves and down the sides of the blouse, plus a ⅛-inch hem at the end of the sleeves and at the bottom of the blouse. When the final pattern is made (if the 10 × 8-inch piece is not the right size), use it to cut out the white fabric. On the wrong side of the fabric, put in the hems on the sleeves, neck,

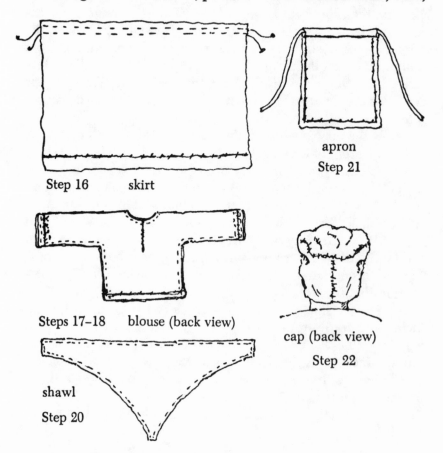

Step 16   skirt

apron
Step 21

Steps 17–18   blouse (back view)

cap (back view)
Step 22

shawl
Step 20

and bottom of blouse, then sew two lines of gathers ⅛ inch apart at the end of the sleeves. Sew up the seams on sleeves and sides on the wrong side.

18. Turn the blouse to the right side and pull over the head. Sew the sides of the back slit together with a blind stitch. Pull gathering stitches together at each wrist and tie threads. Hold the bottom of the blouse in place with a few dots of glue on the clay body. Let glue dry.

19. Pull skirt up over the legs, seam in back, and bring the top over the blouse. Pull gathering stitches tightly at waist and tie threads together.

20. For the shawl, make a tissue paper pattern of a long, blunt-ended triangle. Drape it over the figure's shoulders, pleating it at the top of the shoulders and down the front, and crossing the ends over each other. About ½ inch of the ends should hang below the top of the skirt. The point hangs partway down the back, almost to the top of the skirt. When the final pattern is made, lay it on the black material and cut out. Sew a narrow ⅛-inch hem all around the triangle. Drape and pleat the material over the shoulders and front, tacking if needed. Tack crossed ends to the top of the skirt.

21. Measure and cut a rectangle for the black apron from the tissue paper. The apron is shorter than the skirt, and covers only the front of the skirt. Check for fit, then pin to black fabric and cut out. Sew a ⅛-inch hem on the two sides and bottom of the apron. Then fold the top of the apron over a length of ribbon or cord that is long enough to be tied in a bow at the back of the *santon*. With white glue, hold the apron top over the ribbon or cord, and let glue dry. Put the apron in place over the front of the shawl and top of skirt and tie the cord or ribbon in back.

22. Pull a rectangle of white fabric around the head above the forehead for a high cap, following the drawing. Blind-stitch the back seam; fold top of cap over toward the back and sew in place.

23. For a solid "seat" for the *santon*, fill the plastic pill bottle with sand or small bird gravel, and put the cover back on the bottle. Punch a hole in the plastic cover at the pencil mark using a hot nail (hold nail with a pair of pliers over a stove burner). When the nail is cool, take off the cover and push the nail through

the hole and partway through the cover, the head of the nail on the inside of the cover. Hold the pointed end of the nail firmly as you put the cover back in place so the head and part of the nail are pushed down into the sand or gravel. The pointed end of the nail will be inserted into the body to hold it firmly in place. You have two choices; either drape the skirt over the pill bottle and put nail end in place, or pull the skirt under the legs and make a hole in the back of the skirt, bringing the point of the nail through the skirt and into the body.

24. Try making other *santons*, dressed in other types of clothes. Look in costume books for suggestions.

CHRISTMAS PAPER CRACKERS

Before the invention in the middle 1800s of the "explosive" snapper party favor containing a paper hat and a small toy, these paper crackers were popular in France. Gold or silver paper was loosely wrapped around small candies and tied at each end with ribbon. Two children would tug at the ends until the cracker burst, scattering the candies on the floor and sending the children scrambling to pick them up.

You can make several crackers to pile on a tray near the Christmas tree, so friends can take their chances at a tug-of-war for the sweets inside.

Materials and Tools
gift-wrap paper, gold or silver
small candies, individually wrapped
self-sticking tape, gold, silver, or clear
ribbon, ¼ to ½ inch wide, bright-colored
pencil
ruler
scissors

Directions
1. In this project you are on your own as to the amount of paper, ribbon, and candy you will need. It all depends on the size of each paper cracker, and the number of crackers you are going to make. Gold or silver gift-wrap paper is sold in packages of several sheets or in rolls. As you will have to buy a package or roll, any unused paper can be used for other projects, such as the French Twelfth Night crowns. The amount of candy depends on the size of the paper cracker, the number of pieces in each cracker, and the number of paper crackers you are making.
2. As a suggestion, start with twelve candies and a sheet of paper 10 × 6 inches. Overlap ½ inch on the two 10-inch edges, and hold the edges together with either matching tape or clear tape. Slip the candies through one end so they are in the middle. Twist each end of the paper, 3 inches in from each end. Tie at each twist with ribbon, knotting before tying a bow. Open each end so it flares outward, and push inward on the twisted part so

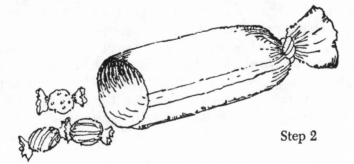

Step 2

the center puffs up. Candies should rattle inside the puffed center section.

3. To break the paper crackers, each child holds a twisted end, then tugs and shakes the cracker until the paper breaks, spilling the candies.

TWELFTH NIGHT CAKE (*Galette des Rois*)

In France there are two types of Twelfth Night cakes. The cake baked in Paris and the area north of the Loire River is called a *galette* and is made from flaky puff pastry, sometimes filled with a layer of marzipan (almond paste). The top is scored in a diamond pattern, then sprinkled with granulated sugar before baking. The cake made in the south of France is a sweet and eggy yeast-risen dough formed into a double ring (a crown), the top decorated before baking with slices of citron and very coarse granulated sugar. Both cakes always contain a dried bean.

Whoever finds the bean in his or her portion of cake becomes the King or Queen for the evening's celebration of Twelfth Night, choosing a Queen or King as partner, and both are crowned with paper crowns. The rest of the evening is filled with dancing, singing, music, and sometimes short plays, ending up with a supper.

Bakers used to make and give away Twelfth Night cakes to their best customers, but were forbidden to do this during the French Revolution, as even the idea of a mock King was considered disloyal. The bakers continued to make the cakes, but they drew the revolutionary liberty cap on top of the cakes. Bakers now sell the cakes for the night's celebration, giving away instead paper king and queen crowns with each cake.

This recipe is for the Parisian cake, and is easy to make as the dough is a packaged, frozen one.

Before you begin, read the Baking instructions in the last chapter.

CAUTION: Never use sharp kitchen equipment or the stove or oven without asking a responsible adult to help you.

Ingredients
    1 package (17½ ounce) frozen puff pastry,
        two ⅛ × 9 × 10-inch sheets
    3½ ounces pure almond paste (sold in
        7-ounce rolls)
    1 egg
    ⅛ teaspoon almond extract
    2½ teaspoons granulated sugar
    large dried bean

Directions
1. Thaw the two sheets of puff pastry for 20 minutes, uncovered, so they can be unfolded.

2. Put almond paste in a small bowl and break it up with a table fork.

3. Beat the egg in a small bowl, and add 1 teaspoon of the beaten egg to the almond paste, plus almond extract. Beat together with the fork, smoothing any lumps with a tablespoon.

4. Turn oven on to 425°. Carefully unfold one sheet of the thawed puff pastry on a lightly floured pastry board. Turn an 8-inch pie plate upside down on the pastry. Place it so the edge is touching two edges of the pastry to give you the largest piece of leftover pastry to make other goodies. Cut around the edges of the pie plate with the point of a knife or serrated cutting wheel.

Steps 4–5

Place the circle of pastry in the middle of an ungreased baking sheet, as this will be the bottom of the cake. Repeat with the other sheet of puff pastry, letting it rest on the pastry board after cutting out the 8-inch circle.

5. On the bottom sheet of pastry, lightly draw a circle with the point of a knife, ¾ inches in from the edge. Spoon almond filling onto the center of this circle, smoothing it to the edge of the line with a spatula or a tablespoon. Put bean into the filling.

6. Brush the ¾-inch margin of the pastry with the beaten egg to which ½ teaspoon of water has been added (see Baking in last chapter for directions). Do not let any egg run over the edge as this may keep the dough from rising. Put the second circle of pastry over the almond filling, matching the edges of the bottom circle. Press edges together with your index finger. Then press the flat of a rounded-end table knife around the edge.

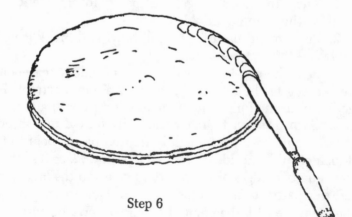

Step 6

7. Brush the top of the pastry with the beaten egg. Press the back of the table knife all around the edges of the circle, making 1-inch-wide "scallops" ½ inch deep. Add a second coat of egg to the top of the pastry and let dry for a minute or two. Then, with the knife point, draw five $\frac{1}{16}$-inch-deep lines across the top circle of pastry. Cross them at right angles with another five lines.

8. Sprinkle top with 2½ teaspoons of granulated sugar, and place baking sheet in the preheated 425° oven. Bake for about 20 minutes or until dough is puffed up and the top is golden brown and shiny, but do not let the bottom burn.

9. Take out of the oven, and remove cake with a wide cake turner to a wire cooling rack. Let cool and serve the same day at room temperature.

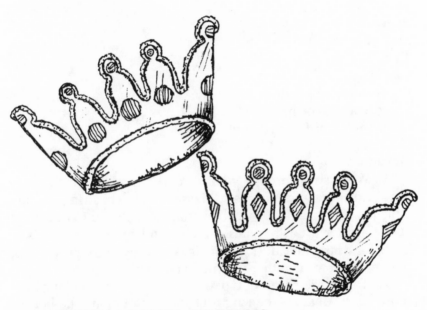

TWELFTH NIGHT CROWNS

Twelfth Night crowns, one for the King and one for the Queen, are made of cardboard covered with gold paper and decorated with bright-colored paper shapes.

Make both crowns large enough to fit any head, then attach the two ends with self-sticking tape when the King and Queen are crowned so the crowns will fit. If you are making the crowns for a grown-up party, then they will be larger than those for a children's party.

Materials and Tools
typewriter paper
self-sticking clear tape
string
thin cardboard or bristol board, 10 × 24 inches
gift-wrap paper, gold
foil paper, red, green, blue
tinsel cord, 25-foot roll, gold
white household glue
facial tissues
pencil
ruler
scissors
4 paper clips
compass
flat watercolor brush, ¾ inch wide
round watercolor brush, #4
small container for mixing glue

Directions
1. Wrap string around your head at the middle of the forehead and cut where ends meet. Measure length of string and add 2 inches. You will need ½-inch overlap at each end to fasten the ends together (which equals 1 inch), and the other inch is to allow for a larger head. If you are making crowns for grown-ups, then measure your father's or mother's head.
2. Tape three sheets of typewriter paper together along their short sides. Measure the length of the crown along the bottom edge of the three sheets of paper, and make a pencil dot. The height for the grown-up crown is about 5 inches. Check the height you want by putting the end of a ruler at the middle of your forehead, then look in the mirror to decide how high the crown should be. Measure this height (or 5 inches) from the bottom of the paper and draw a line; cut along this line so you have a long rectangle of paper.

3. Measure and draw a line 1½ inches in from the bottom of the paper.

4. Fold paper in half crosswise, with the penciled line on the outside; then fold in half again. Now, following the diagram, draw the points of the crown freehand. The point on the right fold is the full height, the point and the half point on the left are shorter, the bottoms of all the points are on the 1½-inch penciled line.

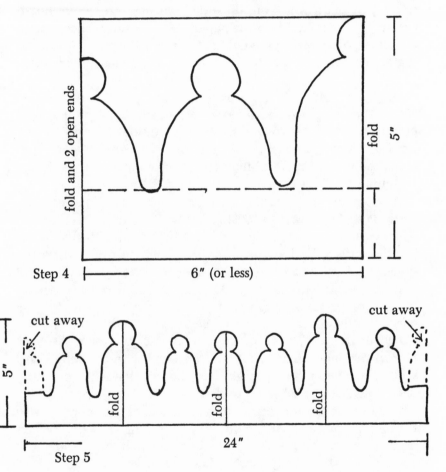

5. Open up the folds and flatten the pattern; at each end there will be a half point. Cut away these two half points at the 1½-inch line.

6. Lay the pattern over half the cardboard or bristol board, trace around the edges, and cut out. Repeat for the second crown on the other half of the board.

7. Next you will cut out the gold paper shapes for the front and back of the two crowns. This is a tricky matter, *so follow directions exactly,* as each point has a separate shape, and the gold paper has to match each shape.

8. Put a small penciled "X" on one board crown, and two small penciled "XXs" on the other crown. Lay both board crowns on the gold side of the paper, "X" sides up. Trace around the edges, then cut out the gold paper along the pencil lines. Put matching X marks on the back of each matching gold paper shape.

9. Turn the two board crowns over and put a small penciled "0" on the "X" crown, and two small penciled "00s" on the "XX" crown. Lay both board crowns on the gold side of the paper, "0" sides up. Trace around the edges, then cut out the gold paper along the pencil lines. Put matching 0 marks on the back of each matching gold shape.

10. Lay the first board crown flat on the newspaper-covered working surface, X side up. Thin out white household glue with a little water, and brush the surface of the board with glue, using the flat brush. If the glue soaks into the board and dries too quickly, add a second coat of glue. Cover with the matching gold paper, the one with a single X. Smooth the surface by laying typewriter paper over the gold paper and slowly drawing the edge of a ruler over the paper while bracing it with your fingers. To cover the full length of the crown, use two more sheets of typewriter paper and repeat the "ironing" with the ruler. This will also squeeze out extra glue, so mop up the edges carefully with facial tissue. Set aside to dry.

11. Repeat the process with the XX side of the other crown, matching it with the XX gold paper covering. Let dry. When both crowns are dry, turn over and add the matching gold paper coverings to the 0 and 00 sides. Let both dry.

12. With the compass, draw seven ⅝-inch circles and seven ⅜-inch circles on the wrong side of the blue foil paper. The ⅝-inch circles will be glued under each point 1½ inches from the bottom, and the ⅜-inch circles will be glued in the center of the circles on top of each point. See diagram for placement. With the white glue and the round brush, cover the back of each circle one by one, and put it in place as it is covered with glue. Let all circles dry.

13. For the other crown, measure and cut seven diamond shapes 1 inch long and ⅝ inch wide from the green foil paper. With the compass, draw seven ⅜-inch circles on the wrong side of the red foil paper. Glue the diamond shapes in the center of each point, and glue the red ⅜-inch circles in the center of the circles on top of each point. Let dry.

14. Glue gold tinsel cord along the top edges of the points and circle tops, and along the lower edges of the two crowns, except the two overlap areas at each end. Let dry.

15. When the King and Queen have been chosen, fit the crowns on their heads, overlapping the straight sections and holding them in place with two paper clips. Slip off the crowns; trim away any excess overlap, then hold the ends firmly in place with two lengths of clear, self-sticking tape inside and out.

Germany

✦✦✦

In some sections of Germany, from the first Sunday of Advent to Twelfth Night Sunday, a candle is lighted each Sunday on a seven-branched candlestick: one candle on the first Sunday, two on the second, and so on. At this time the family gathers to sing carols. In other parts of Germany the homes have a circle of greenery on a table with four candles placed around the circle. Each candle in turn is lighted on the four Sundays of Advent before Christmas Day.

For centuries the Yule Log has been lighted at Christmastime to scare away Father Frost, a custom that goes back to pagan days. It was also in Germany that pictures were supposedly first drawn of the red-coated, bearded Santa Klaus and his reindeer.

From Germany, too, came the first decorated Christmas tree. Legend has it that in the early sixteenth century, Martin Luther decorated the first Christmas tree, fixing small candles to the branch ends of an evergreen tree. Through the years the decorations grew more and more elaborate, and were kept from year to year. The tree was set up and decorated behind a locked door, and presents were put around the base and piled on nearby tables. Then, after dinner on Christmas Eve, the door was thrown open and the children rushed in to admire the tree with its glittering decorations and flickering candles and to find their brightly wrapped packages.

ADVENT CALENDAR

Generations of German children have received or made Advent Calendars that mark the days from December 1 to December 24. They are illustrated with brightly colored Christmas scenes, snow-covered villages or towns, farm scenes, or Santa's workshop. There are twenty-four numbered doors, windows, roofs, trees, haystacks, and boxes. The numbers are scattered hit-or-miss over the scene so they have to be searched out, and when the right number of the day of the month is found and the flap lifted up, there is the day's surprise. It is a small picture of a toy or doll, a Christmas package, cakes or cookies, small pet animals, or all sorts of tiny Christmas scenes.

Make a calendar for your best friend. Before you begin, read the sections on Paper Gluing and Painting in the last chapter.

Materials and Tools
typewriter paper, 2 sheets
clear, self-sticking tape
lead-pencil transfer paper (see last chapter)
heavy white paper or medium-surface, lightweight
    bristol board, 15 × 20 inches (a standard size sheet)
fine-line pen, permanent black
eraser
crayons, or felt-tipped marking pens, or acrylic paints,
    red, green, blue, yellow, brown
white household glue
facial tissues
cord, 16 inches, black, red, or natural
pencil
ruler
large scissors
small pointed manicure scissors
craft knife
flat nylon brush, ½ inch wide
round nylon brushes, #2 and #5
small containers for mixing glue and acrylic paints
hole punch, nail, or skewer
gift-wrap seals (optional, see Variation)

Top Sheet   Enlarge to ½" squares

Directions

1. Enlarge both drawings on the typewriter paper, using the grid method.

2. With the scissors or craft knife and ruler, cut the heavy paper or bristol board into two 8½ × 10-inch sheets. Attach each drawing to a sheet with two pieces of self-sticking tape at the top corners, half the tape on the back of the sheet, the other half stuck to the front of the drawing.

3. Slip the lead-pencil transfer paper under one drawing, lead-pencil side down. Trace over all lines with a pencil, bearing down on the point so the drawing will be transferred. When you have finished, carefully lift the bottom end of the drawing and transfer paper and look below to make sure all lines have been

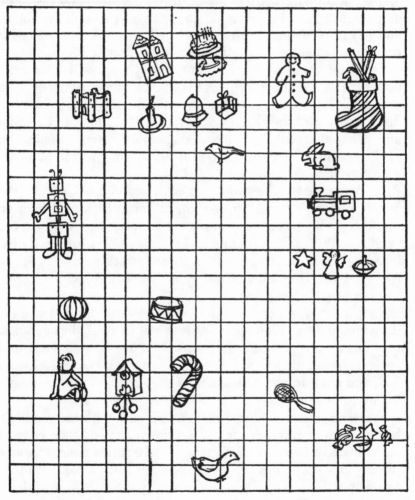

Bottom Sheet   Enlarge to ½" squares

followed. If not, replace the drawing and transfer paper and add the missing lines. Then remove the transfer paper and place it under the other drawing, tracing all lines of the second drawing. Remove transfer paper and the typewriter-paper drawings.

4. If you are coloring the transferred drawings with crayons or felt-tipped marking pens, go over all the pencil lines on the top drawing with a fine-line pen, then erase any pencil lines that are showing. Color the buildings any color you wish; the chimneys are red or brown, the trees green, the sky is blue, and the snow on the hillside can be lightly shaded with blue around the houses and trees. After the coloring is finished, add the numbers with the fine-line pen as shown on the pattern drawing.

5. If you are using acrylic paint, mix it with water; then use both the flat and round brushes to put on a thin covering of color so you can still see the transferred pencil lines. After the paint has dried, go over all the pencil lines with the fine-line pen. Brighten any areas that need it, like trees, roofs, barn, ribbons on packages, doors, and window shutters. Then add the numbers with the fine-line pen.

6. When the top sheet has been colored and dried, cut out the openings along the solid lines, using the craft knife and ruler on the straight lines and the manicure scissors on the small curved openings. With the craft knife and ruler, lightly score the dotted lines (see Paper in the last chapter for scoring directions). Lightly fold back each flap only part way, so you can follow the directions in Step 7.

7. Put the top sheet over the second sheet and check the pencil drawings underneath to be sure they show through the openings, then make any needed corrections. Remove bottom sheet and color the small drawings, following the directions in Steps 4 and 5. If you are using acrylic paint, let drawing dry well before going on to Step 8.

8. Mix white glue with a little water, and with the round #5 brush, thinly cover a ¼-inch space down each 10-inch edge of both sheets of the calendar. Press the two sheets together, wipe off any glue that oozes out along the edges with a piece of facial tissue, put flaps back in position, and place calendar under a large book (a telephone book will do, with a couple of heavier books on top).

9. When the calendar is dry, remove from book weights. Put a hole in each top corner with a hole punch, nail, or skewer. Push each end of the cord through a hole and tie in a knot.

Variation: Instead of using the small drawings, cut out small pictures from gift-wrap seals and paste in position on the bottom sheet.

TINY CHRISTMAS ANGEL

In Germany there is always an angel on the Christmas tree, hung on a branch or perched at the very top of the tree. Angels were carved from wood and painted, or made of colored wax with spun-glass wings, or fashioned of gold paper pleated and folded into shape. This tiny angel is made of wooden beads and white ribbon, light enough to hang on the very end of a branch.

Materials and Tools
typewriter paper
round wooden beads: 2 natural color, ½ or ⅝ inches in
    diameter; 1 blue or other color, ¼ or ⅜ inches in diameter
grosgrain ribbon, 2½ × 7 inches, white
cardboard or bristol board, ½ × ⅝ inches, white
contact cement
felt-tipped marking pen, black
jute twine, ¼ × 3 inches
sewing thread, white, tan
pencil
ruler
scissors
needle

Directions

1. Cement the three beads together with the smaller colored bead in the center (see Gluing in the last chapter for directions on contact cement).

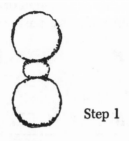

Step 1

2. Sew a row of gathering stitches close to one 7-inch edge of the grosgrain ribbon, starting and finishing ¼ inch in from each 2½-inch end. Sew the two 2½-inch ends together in a ¼-inch seam using a strengthened stitch; then turn the ribbon over so the seam is inside (see Sewing in the last chapter for directions). Pull on the thread of the gathering stitches, fitting the gathered top of the skirt into the space between the lowest wooden bead and the smaller colored bead in the center, tucking the gathers inside the skirt. Thread the needle and finish off the thread.

3. Transfer the wing pattern to the typewriter paper by the grid method. Cut out pattern, place on white cardboard or bristol board, then trace and cut two pieces. Put a drop of contact cement on one end of each wing, and two drops in the center of the back of the colored bead in line with the back seam of the skirt. When cement is clear, press the wings into position, angling them up and out to each side.

Wing

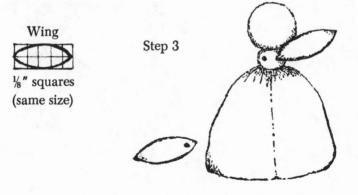

⅛" squares
(same size)

Step 3

4. Cut a 4-inch length of white thread, fold it in half, and cement the two ends to the center back of the large upper bead as a hanging loop.

5. Cut the 3-inch length of jute twine into four equal pieces. Separate the strands, and cement to the top and back of the large upper bead, forming a center part. Keep the hanging thread upright so it does get caught in the strands. Gather together about ¼ to ⅜ inches of strands at each end and wrap a length of tan thread around them, tying it so the ends stick out from the head on each side.

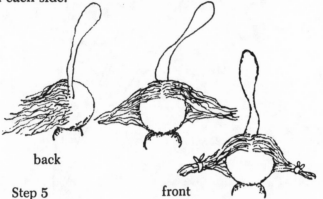

back

Step 5   front

6. Add eyes, nose, and mouth with the black felt-tipped pen. The angel is now ready to hang on the tree, or on a Christmas package.

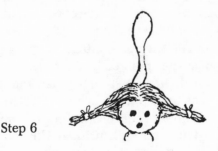

Step 6

Variation: Do not cement a hanging thread on the head. Instead, make several angels to decorate the Christmas table, placing them at each place; they will stand alone, supported by the stiff skirt. Or add the angels to a crèche scene.

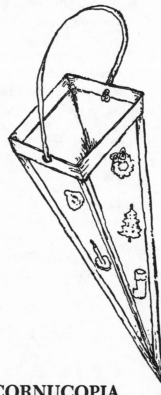

SQUARE-TOP CORNUCOPIA

Decorated cornucopias hanging from the green branches of German Christmas trees at the turn of the century held sweet candies, tiny cookies, *pfeffernüsse* (peppernuts), and sometimes a small trinket or coin. The surprise contents were eagerly anticipated by the children as they pointed to a cornucopia high on the tree or reached for one lower down. They had made the paper cornucopias, but it was their parents who had filled them.

Each white, thin-cardboard cornucopia, edges bound with red or green ribbon and trimmed with printed Christmas stickers, was hung by a ribbon loop. Sometimes the white cardboard was covered with bright-colored paper with contrasting ribbon edging the four corners.

If you do not have white-surfaced cardboard, bristol, or illustration board, then cover gray or tan cardboard with white or colored Con-Tact paper after the cornucopia has been cut out and the four corners scored. Use colored self-sticking tape to bind the corners and top. Christmas-package seals are sold in small plastic bags wherever gift wrappings are sold.

The materials listed below are for one cornucopia.

Materials and Tools
typewriter paper
white-surfaced cardboard, bristol, or illustration board,
   8 × 10⅞ inches
self-sticking tape, 60 inches, ½ inch wide, red or green
Christmas-package seals
ribbon, ½ × 12 inches
cardboard, gray or tan (see Variation)
Con-Tact paper, white or colored (see Variation)
pencil
ruler
scissors
craft knife

Directions
1. Enlarge the pattern on typewriter paper by the grid method. Cut out.

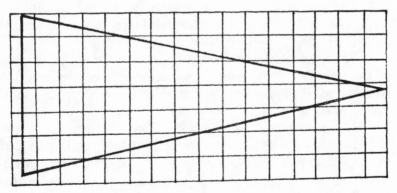

Step 1   Enlarge to ½″ squares

2. Measure and cut out a piece of cardboard, bristol, or illustration board 8 × 10⅞ inches. On the white side measure and rule a pencil line 3¼ inches in from the left 8-inch side. Lay the right edge of the triangle against this line, broad end at top. Trace around edges. Move pattern to the right, matching top and bottom with the left side of the pattern against the right side of the traced triangle. Trace around the top and right side of the pattern. Move the triangle to the right, and repeat the tracing for the third and then the fourth triangle. You'll now have four joined triangles in a fan shape.

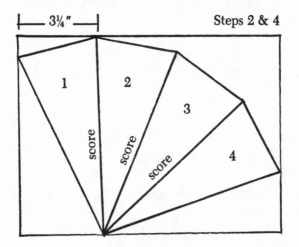

3. Cut out around the outer three edges of the fan shape with scissors or craft knife. If using the craft knife, brace it against the ruler for a clean, even cut.

4. Score (see Paper in the last chapter) the three joining lines of the triangles, using ruler and craft knife. Slowly bend each section back from the shallow scored line so the two free edges of the cornucopia meet.

5. Cut a 7⅞-inch length of colored self-sticking tape. Press a ¼-inch-wide strip down one open edge of the cornucopia. Bring the two sides together, so they touch all the way down. Smooth the other ¼-inch half of the tape on the opposite side of the opening. Repeat taping over the three scored corners.

6. For the hanging loop, cut a 12-inch length of ribbon. Fasten ½ inch of each end of the ribbon to the center top of facing triangles, using a 1-inch length of tape across each ribbon end.

7. Add a strip of tape around the top of all four sides of the cornucopia, covering the two 1-inch pieces. Then add a matching length around the inside top of all four sides.

8. Glue Christmas package seals here and there on the sides. Fill the cornucopia with candies and a small surprise, then hang it on a tree branch. Make as many cornucopias as you want, for your own tree and for friends.

Variation: If you are using ordinary gray or tan cardboard, then cover with white or colored Con-Tact paper following the manufacturer's directions. Hold the two open edges together with a ½-inch-wide strip of Con-Tact paper. Bind all four edges and top with contrasting colored tape, adding ribbon hanger and seals as in Steps 5 through 8.

Cornucopias can be made in any size, smaller or larger than the measurements given in this project.

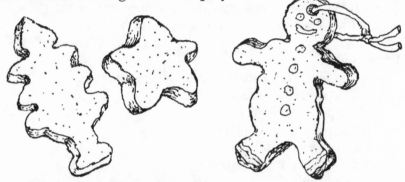

HONEY SPICE COOKIES (*Nuremberg Lebkuchen*)

The Nuremberg Fair has been held in the Market Square of that German city for four hundred years. It lasts for three weeks, from early in December to Christmas Eve, and there are booths where Christmas toys and decorations are sold. Other booths are hung with sausages and cheeses, and still others are piled high with Christmas cakes, breads, and cookies. There are processions and choral singing of carols; church bells ring, pageants are performed, and after dark the area is lighted with medieval lanterns. It is a bustling, joyous beginning of the Christmas season.

The spice cookies (*Lebkuchen*), made by generations of Nuremberg bakers, are sold at the Fair and shipped all over the world. Because they contain no shortening, they will keep for weeks and can be made long before Christmas. They need only a moistened paper towel or a quartered apple put into the cookie tin to soften them. The dough is formed into many shapes with cookie cutters: stars, Christmas trees, fluted rounds, hearts, bells, and even "gingerbread" men. They are finished with either a baked-on egg glaze, a thin white lemon icing, or a thin chocolate glaze.

If you like, put a hole in the top of the bells, stars, trees, and men before baking so they can be hung by a cord on the tree in traditional fashion. Or put them all in a tin, and a day or two before serving moisten the cookies, then serve with mulled cider or milk, or just munch on them.

Before you begin, read section on Baking in the last chapter.

CAUTION: Never use sharp kitchen equipment or the stove or oven without asking a responsible adult to help you.

Ingredients
> ½ cup chopped blanched and toasted almonds
> (use slivered almonds)
> 1½ cups sifted flour
> ¼ teaspoon ground cloves
> 1 teaspoon ground cinnamon
> ⅛ teaspoon ground nutmeg
> pinch of salt
> 6 tablespoons honey
> 1½ tablespoons molasses
> 5 tablespoons plus 1 teaspoon dark brown sugar
> 4 tablespoons chopped candied citron
> ¼ teaspoon lemon extract
> ½ teaspoon orange extract
> ⅛ teaspoon baking soda
> ¾ teaspoon hot water
> 1 egg

cookie cutters: star, tree, heart, bell, fluted

Directions

1. Blanch the almonds or buy skinless blanched and slivered almonds. Put skinned almonds on a pan and into a 350° oven, turning often until light brown. Remove from oven, cool, and chop into small pieces, $\frac{1}{16}$ inch or a little more.

2. Sift flour, cloves, cinnamon, nutmeg, and salt together into a bowl.

3. In a larger bowl, mix the honey and molasses together, then add the dark brown sugar and mix well. Add the lemon and orange extract and stir into the mixture.

4. Beat the egg in a small bowl. Add about $\frac{1}{3}$ the beaten egg to the mixture. Cover the rest of the egg and place in the refrigerator as it will be used to brush the cookies before baking.

5. Cut citron into small pieces, about $\frac{1}{16}$-inch long, and dust with a pinch of flour to separate pieces. Add to mixture.

6. Mix the hot water with the baking soda, and stir into mixture.

7. Add flour, half a cup at a time, stirring with a wooden spoon until each addition is well mixed in. Then add nuts and stir. The dough will be thick and stiff.

8. Form dough into a ball, put inside a plastic bag, tie the end of the bag, and place in the refrigerator overnight. This gives the flavorings a chance to blend together.

9. Roll out the dough the next day on a floured board, or between two sheets of floured wax paper to $\frac{1}{4}$-inch thickness. Cut out cookies with your choice of cookie cutter. This amount of dough will make about thirty-six 2-inch stars, or ten $3\frac{1}{2}$-inch-long Christmas trees, or six to eight 5-inch-long gingerbread men (dough is rolled a little thicker for the gingerbread men). Or you can make an assortment of shapes, depending on how many cookie cutter shapes you have. After the first cutting out of the cookies, gather up the scraps, reroll, and cut out more cookies. Repeat until all the dough is used.

10. Place cookies on a greased cookie sheet. Brush with the rest of the egg mixed with $\frac{1}{4}$ teaspoon of water, and bake in a preheated 350° oven for *not more than* 15 minutes. Remove from oven to a rack and let cool.

11. Make icing with confectioners' sugar mixed with a little lemon juice and a couple of drops of lemon extract. Add eyes, mouth, buttons, and shoe-line at the end of each leg to the gingerbread men with this icing.

Variation: If you want to hang the cookies on the Christmas tree, make a round hole with a skewer in the top of the cookies, just after they have been cut out from the dough. After baking and cooling, add a loop of gold cord to each cookie, tying the ends of the cord together. Do not ice these cookies.

WOOLLY SHEEP

Christmas crib scenes, some simple and some elaborate, are set up in many churches and homes throughout the world. Animals are an important part of the stable scene: cows, asses, sheep, and the camels of the Three Wise Men. Animals have been carved from wood, formed with clay and baked, woven of braided straw, or sewn together from scraps of fabric or fur and stuffed. The fabric was sometimes covered with loops of the "raw" wool (called roving) before it was spun into yarn.

This woolly sheep from Germany is formed over a cardboard tube base, with loops of twisted wool glued to the base. Use very thick knitting yarn, either wool or acrylic, lightly twisting several strands together. The head and legs of the original sheep were covered with tan burlap, and the ears and feet made of black felt. Tan felt is easier to handle as it does not ravel the way burlap does, and it can be bought in a smaller piece. Pieces of the same felt used for ears and feet can be colored with a black felt-tipped pen. Or use any scraps of tan cloth you might find in a scrap bag.

Materials and Tools
cardboard tube, 1½ × 4 inches
10 pipe cleaners
felt-tipped pen, black
tissue paper or newspaper
white household glue
masking tape, ¾ inch wide
cork, ¾ × 1¾ inches, or styrofoam block (same size)
thin nail, less than ⅛ inch in diameter, 2¼ inches long
acrylic paint, white
felt, 8 × 10-inch piece, tan
2 small rubber bands
button and carpet thread
knitting yarn, about ¼ inch in diameter, up to 10 yards
pencil
ruler
scissors
skewer, less than ⅛ inch in diameter, 5¾ inches long
  (optional)
craft knife
straight pins
flat nylon brush, ½ inch wide
small containers for mixing glue and acrylic paint

Directions
  1. Measure, then cut with the craft knife, a 4-inch length from a cardboard tube, from a roll of paper towels or bathroom tissue.

Step 1   Step 2

  2. Attach the center core for each pipe cleaner leg to the bottom of the cardboard tube. For the two front legs, make two pencil dots, ¾ inch in from one end of the tube and 1 inch apart. For the back legs, make two dots, ½ inch in from the other end of

the tube and 1 inch apart. With the skewer or nail, make a hole in the cardboard tube at each of these pencil marks. Then make four more holes, each ¼ inch toward the center of the tube from the first set of holes.

3. Make a mark with the felt-tipped pen ¾ inch from one end of a pipe cleaner. Push this end through a first hole, well inside the tube. Reach inside and bend the pipe cleaner at the ¾-inch mark until the point is opposite the second hole. Push the point through the second hole and pull downward on the pipe cleaner. Wrap the short end around the other part of the pipe cleaner, close to the tube. Repeat with three other pipe cleaners.

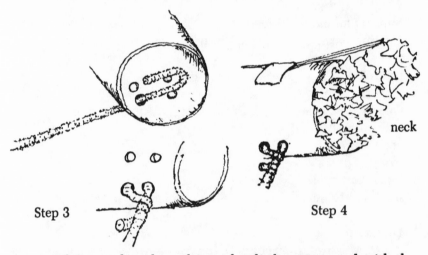

neck

Step 3   Step 4

4. Thin out the white glue with a little water, and with the brush cover the inside of the cardboard tube and the tops of pipe cleaners with one or two coats of glue. Crumple tissue paper or newspaper into cylinders that will fit inside the tube, smearing them with glue before pushing them in with the pencil. Keep pushing crumpled paper inside the tube until it is solidly packed, holding the palm of one hand against the back opening of the tube so the paper will stay inside. For the neck, crumple a fairly large piece partway inside the tube and partway outside, squeezing the outside piece into a rounded, oblong neck 1 inch long and 1 inch in diameter with glue to hold the paper together. Angle the neck slightly upward, and hold in position with a strip of masking tape attached to the top of the cardboard tube.

Step 5

5. For the head, carve one end of the cork into a flat cone shape using the craft knife. The flat side is the bottom of the head. Broaden the wide end with tissue paper wrapped around and around, spreading glue between layers. Taper the strips of paper down to the cone-shaped nose. Let dry.

6. Insert the nail at an angle near the bottom of the back end of the cork. Thrust the nail into the neck and wrap the neck with masking tape, bringing strips up over the top, sides, and bottom of the head. Body, neck, and head should be solidly attached together.

nail

Step 6

7. Mix acrylic paint with a little water and cover tube and masking tape with a thin coat of paint. Let dry.

8. Bend all four pipe cleaners back on themselves at a point 2 inches from the bottom of the cardboard tube. Check whether

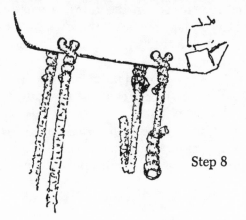

Step 8

the sheep will stand evenly on the legs, and adjust length of legs if necessary. Then, one at a time, wind the bent back extra length of pipe cleaner closely around each 2-inch length. Add extra pipe cleaners to finish winding the legs, cutting them off when the top of the leg is reached.

9. To make the pattern for the felt head-covering, cut a piece of tissue paper 3½ × 5 inches, slightly rounded on one 5-inch side. Stretch it over the head, straight side at the back of the head, and fold the paper underneath the head. Trim away any excess paper. Remove tissue paper from the head and pin to the felt, then cut out the felt head-covering. Spread glue over the head and the matching side of the felt. Place felt in position, adding glue to the folds. Stick pins straight through the folds and into the cork, adding one or two small rubber bands around the head until the glue dries; then remove pins and rubber bands.

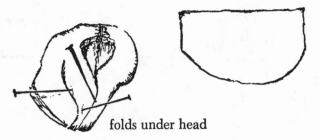

folds under head

Step 9

10. For the felt leg-coverings, first measure the circumference of a leg by wrapping thread around the leg, adding a ⅛-inch overlap, then lay thread on the ruler to measure it. Cut four pieces of felt to this width, each 2 inches long. Cover pipe cleaners and matching side of felt with glue, wrap felt around the legs with the overlapping seam at the back of each leg. Stick pins straight into the seams to hold them in place until the glue dries.

11. Follow the drawings in covering the body, top of head, and top of legs with knitting yarn. The amount needed depends on the thickness of the yarn. If it is ¼ inch in diameter, you will have to use two strands twisted lightly together for the back and sides of the body, with the separate strands pulled apart for softness.

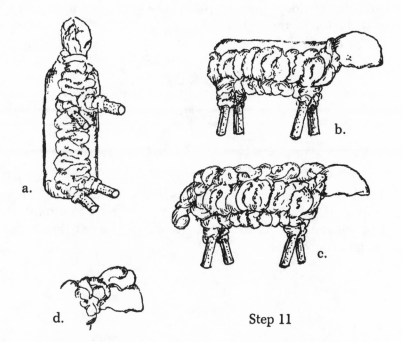

a.

b.

c.

d.   Step 11

a. First cover the bottom of the tube (a narrow rectangle that includes the legs) with two layers of yarn in tight 2¼-inch-long S curves, gluing the first layer to the tube. The second layer is glued only at the curved ends. Cross yarn over between the legs, and make four turns around the top of each leg, covering about ¾ inch of the leg, gluing the yarn in place.

b. For each side, pull the double strands apart for broad, soft 1¼-inch-wide S curves, first layer glued to the tube, upper layer lightly glued. Continue S curves of yarn across the chest between the head and legs. Bring side S curves of yarn around to the back, rounding out this area.

c. The top of the sheep's body is a double thickness of soft 1¼- to 1½-inch S curves, first layer glued to the tube, upper layer lightly glued. Twist two strands of yarn together to form a 2-inch-long tail. Tuck ¼ inch under the top yarn covering at the back, and glue in place.

d. Continue the center back layer around the neck, wrapping the yarn around several times, and making a double layer of yarn. Add two loops on each side of the head, and a long, thick one at the top of the head.

Step 12

12. From the felt, cut two half ovals ⅝ × ¾ inches for the ears, and four strips ⅛ inch wide and long enough to go around the bottom of each leg. Color them black with the felt-tipped pen. Glue into place.

Greece

✧ ✧ ✧

Christmas is a religious holiday and one of feasting after weeks of fasting. On Christmas Eve, children go through the village knocking on doors and singing the *Kalanda*, proclaiming the birth of Christ. Boys accompany the singing by banging on small metal triangles and clay drums.

On Christmas Day there is a feast which includes sweet breads and special cookies, and for these, precious white flour and sugar are used. The housewives, having kept sprigs of the Greek small-leaved basil alive in a bowl of water, wrap a sprig around a small wooden cross, dip the leaves in the water, and sprinkle it about the rooms to keep the mischievous goblins away from the house. Since the Greek church bases its holy days on the old calendar, Christmas is celebrated one week later than the European one.

On Epiphany day, the twelfth day after Christmas day, the ships in the harbors are blessed by a priest in the name of St. Nicholas, the patron saint of sailors, so he will watch over each ship and bring it safely through storms to the home harbor. Ships' whistles blow, church bells ring, a cross is thrown into the water and sailors dive in to retrieve it.

The legends about Saint Nicholas have spread to many countries. He takes many forms, and his "day" is December 6, which is the day he died in 342 A.D. He was born in Lycia, on the southern coast of what is now Turkey, and eventually he became Bishop of Myra. Many miracles and stories are told about him:

the ransoming of three kidnapped girls, the arrival of grain ships during a famine, protecting the poor and the sailors at sea.

When he died he was buried in Myra, but his body was spirited away from Myra in the eleventh century and taken to Bari in southeastern Italy on the Adriatic Sea, where he is buried in the Church of St. Nicholas. Pilgrims came from all over Europe to the church to pray to Saint Nicholas during the Norman-French occupation of that part of Italy at the time of the Crusades, and it was in this way that the fame of St. Nicholas spread all over Europe.

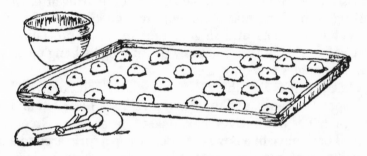

COURAMBIADES (*Shortbread Christmas Cookies*)

In Greece, sweet buttery cookies covered heavily with powdered sugar flavored with rose or almond essence are part of the Christmas feast. Butter, sugar, and white flour were once expensive and rare in a country that depended on olive oil, honey, and coarse dark flours, so these cookies were a once-a-year luxury at Christmastime. A whole clove is stuck in the center of each cookie to remind everyone of the spices brought by the Magi to the Christ Child. A very similar cookie in the shape of a quarter moon is made in Austria at Christmastime.

This recipe is for two dozen cookies; double all ingredients if you want to make four dozen cookies.

Before beginning, read Baking in the last chapter.

CAUTION: Never use sharp kitchen equipment or the stove or oven without asking a responsible adult to help you.

Ingredients
¼ pound unsalted butter or margarine
1 teaspoon solid white vegetable shortening
½ teaspoon almond extract or rose essence flavoring
¼ teaspoon baking powder
¾ cup flour
2 tablespoons half-and-half or light cream
¾ cup confectioner's sugar
½ teaspoon almond extract or rose essence
24 cloves

Directions
1. Let butter stay in a bowl at room temperature for 1 to 1½ hours. Then cream (beat with a tablespoon) until fluffy. Add the solid vegetable shortening, mixing well. Add ½ teaspoon of flavoring.

2. Mix baking powder with the flour and sift over the butter mixture, alternating with the half-and-half. Mix well into a very soft dough. Cover bowl with clear plastic food wrap, and place in the refrigerator overnight so dough will stiffen.

3. The next day, before taking the bowl out of the refrigerator, sift ¾ cup of confectioner's sugar into a bowl and sprinkle with the other ½ teaspoon of rose or almond flavoring, stirring lightly with a fork. Let stand for 15 to 20 minutes to dry.

4. Cut an 18-inch piece of aluminum foil and place it on a flat surface, turning up ½ inch around all the edges. Put flavored confectioner's sugar in a sieve and cover surface of foil with the sugar to a depth of ⅛ inch. You'll have sugar left over and will use it later.

5. Take dough out of the refrigerator. Grease cookie sheet with vegetable shortening. Set oven for 400°. Scoop out dough with a measuring teaspoon, placing dough on cookie sheet about an inch apart. Slightly smooth the mounds and stick a clove in the center of each cookie. When sheet is filled, place in the oven for 12 minutes or until the bottom of each cookie is brown (tops will not be brown).

6. Take cookie sheet out of the oven and immediately transfer cookies to the aluminum foil with a broad cake turner. Sift sugar over the tops of the cookies. Let them stand until cold, as they will break if moved when they are warm. When cold, place cookies on a cake rack and put rack over the foil. Dust more sugar over the tops (use resifted sugar from the foil.)

Step 7

7. Pack away in an airtight box with wax paper between the layers. They are best if kept for a day. Resift leftover confectioner's sugar and put into a covered jar or plastic bag; dust it over cookies just before serving.

Holland

❖ ❖ ❖

In Holland, it is St. Nicholas (*Sinterklass* or Saint Nicholaus) who brings gifts to children on his day, December 6. Wearing his bishop's cape and hat he carries three bags of presents for good children, or he is sometimes followed by a cart filled with gifts. In the introduction to the United States celebrations, you can read about how *Sinterklass* became Santa Claus.

Gifts in Holland are often enclosed in many wrappings, each layer being a different color or even a different material, so that half the fun of gift-giving is in the wrapping, and then in the unwrapping.

Christmas Day itself is a religious time of churchgoing and a family feast. During the Christmas season there was an old custom of young people going through the streets singing carols and carrying stars on long poles, and this was called star-singing. It is a custom carried out in many European countries.

DUTCH "WOODEN" SHOE

In Holland, Saint Nicholas (*Sinterklaas*) and his partner Black Peter are the givers of gifts to children on Saint Nicholas Eve, December 6. They go from house to house, Saint Nicholas riding his white horse and carrying his three sacks of gifts for good children. Peter, walking beside him, carries switches and chunks of coal for the bad children.

Before going to bed on Saint Nicholas Eve, children put a wooden shoe on the windowsill, filled with straw for the white horse. In the morning the straw is gone and the shoe is filled with sweets and small gifts, all topped with an almond paste filled cookie in the shape of the child's first-name initial. Directions for making the cookie are on page 69.

Carving a wooden shoe is a very difficult project, so this shoe is made of cardboard covered with papier-mâché and painted a soft yellow.

Materials and Tools
typewriter paper
cardboard or bristol board, 12½ × 16 inches
papier-mâché (see Papier-mâché in the last chapter
   for directions)
masking tape
sandpaper
acrylic polymer gloss medium
acrylic paint, yellow (or chrome yellow and white)
facial tissues
pencil
ruler
scissors
flat nylon brush, 1 inch wide
small container for mixing paint

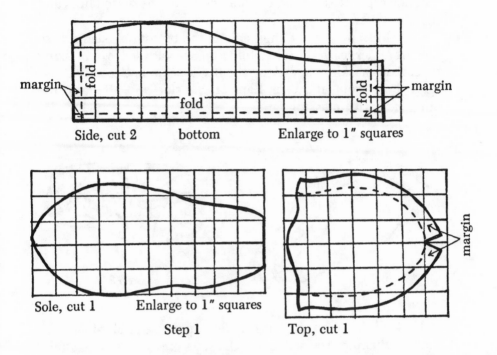

Side, cut 2   bottom   Enlarge to 1″ squares

Sole, cut 1   Enlarge to 1″ squares

Step 1   Top, cut 1

Directions

1. Enlarge patterns on the typewriter paper by the grid method, first making a large enough sheet by fastening separate pieces together with masking tape. Cut out the three patterns. Lay patterns over the cardboard, trace around the edges, and cut out with the scissors. In tracing the side patterns, reverse one pattern and leave off its front and back flaps. Score along the dotted lines using the craft knife and ruler (see Paper in the last chapter for directions). Every ¾ inch along the margins of the sides and

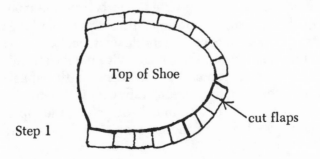

Top of Shoe

cut flaps

Step 1

the shoe top, measure and cut lines between the dotted lines and the outside edges.

2. Fold flaps at right angles along the bottom of each side so they fit underneath the sole. Hold in place with strips of masking tape. Add masking tape along the inside seam between sole and sides. Fold front and back flaps of one side and attach to the other side with masking tape.

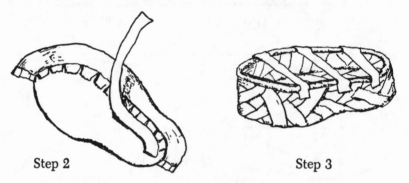

Step 2   Step 3

3. Read directions for making and applying papier-mâché in the last chapter. You will cover the sides and sole with a ¼-inch layer of papier-mâché on both the outside and inside. First, add a ⅛-inch thickness of papier-mâché to the cardboard. Let it dry a bit, then add the second ⅛ inch and let dry. If sides lean outward, straighten them up, and hold in place with lengths of masking tape stretched between them (see diagram).

4. Cover both surfaces of the shoe top with papier-mâché (except the flaps), following directions in Step 3. Just before the papier-mâché is completely dry, place the top in position over the sides and curve it to fit the sides. Let the top dry in position, flaps folded down on the outside of the two sides.

5. Remove the masking-tape supports from the shoe. Hold the flaps of the shoe top in position with strips of masking tape; also add strips of tape to cover the inside seam between top and sides. Cover masking tape on the outside with papier-mâché, blending the strips over the top and sides. Repeat with papier-mâché on the inside, covering the masking tape over the seam. Add strips of papier-mâché to form a rounded edge along the top of the sides and the exposed edge of the shoe top. Let dry thoroughly.

6. When dry, sandpaper all surfaces inside and out until smooth. Brush off the dust with facial tissues.

7. With the acrylic polymer gloss medium and the flat brush, cover all the outside surfaces of the sides and tops. When dry, turn the shoe over and cover the bottom of the sole with the medium, and let dry. Turn the shoe right side up, and cover the inside of the shoe with the medium. When thoroughly dry, cover the shoe with a second coat of the medium and let dry.

8. Mix the light-yellow paint with the gloss medium in the small container. If using a strong chrome-yellow paint, add some white paint to lighten the color. Paint the inside of the shoe and the outside of the sides and top, using the flat brush. Let paint dry before turning over the shoe to paint the bottom of the sole. Let dry, then add a second coat of paint. Set shoe aside until completely dry. If you want a very shiny surface, then cover the whole shoe with a coat of the gloss medium on top of the yellow paint. When surface is hard and dry, the shoe can be filled with goodies.

INITIAL LETTER COOKIES

Here is the recipe for the initial letter cookies that Saint Nicholas puts on top of each wooden shoe he has filled with presents. The cookies filled with almond paste are made in many sizes from two to eight inches long.

This recipe makes only a few cookies, but after you have made it and want to make more, then double or triple all the ingredients. It is always best to make a small amount of a new recipe to test it out.

Before you begin, read the section on Baking in the last chapter.

CAUTION: Never use sharp kitchen equipment or the stove or oven without asking a responsible adult to help you.

Ingredients
½ cup flour
4 tablespoons butter or margarine
1 tablespoon cold water
½ cup almond paste
½ egg beaten with ½ teaspoon water (see Tip
   at end of recipe)
¼ teaspoon vanilla
2 to 3 drops almond extract

Directions
1. Sift flour into a small mixing bowl. Cut butter or margarine into small pieces and add them to the flour. With your fingertips, lightly blend the pieces into the flour until the mixture is like cornmeal.

2. Add the tablespoon of cold water mixed with the vanilla to the flour mixture, stirring it with a table fork. If you cannot form a ball with the dough, then add a little more water, ½ teaspoon at a time, but do not let the dough get sticky and soft.

3. Gather the dough into a ball, wrap in plastic wrap, and put in the refrigerator for 30 minutes to chill.

4. Place dough between two sheets of lightly floured wax paper, and roll out to ⅛-inch thickness, keeping as near a rectangular shape as possible, with one side 5 inches long. Remove top sheet of paper carefully, and cut dough into strips, 5 inches long and 2½ inches wide.

5. Put almond paste in a bowl and add the almond extract, mixing it in with a fork. Taste a little bit to see if the flavor is strong enough. If not, add another drop or two of flavoring.

Lightly roll paste with the palms of your hands on a clean sheet of wax paper, forming thin rolls ⅜ inches in diameter and 4½ inches long.

6. Lift up one length of dough, place almond paste roll in the center, and bring dough around it. Close the long edge and each end with water, making sure they are well sealed. Repeat with rest of dough. Reroll any scraps into another strip.

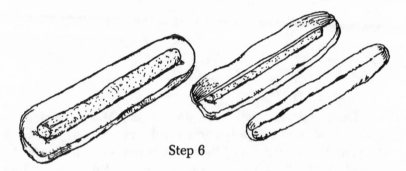

Step 6

7. Carefully form the rolls into letters of your choice, seam on the bottom. As you finish, place each one on a buttered baking sheet. When all the letters have been made and transferred to the baking sheet, brush them with the beaten egg. Bake in a 400° oven for 20 minutes. Check then to see if dough is light brown, and if not, check again in 5 minutes. Remove from oven when done, and with a spatula transfer cookies to a rack to cool.

Tip: Beat egg and water with fork, then measure it out, one measuring tablespoon at a time, into two separate containers. When you are finished, each container will hold half an egg.

Italy

❖ ❖ ❖

The official date of December 25 for the Mass to celebrate Christ's birthday was finally chosen in Rome early in the fourth century. Before that, it had been celebrated on other dates including January 6, which is now known as Epiphany, Three Kings' Day, or Twelfth Night. This is the day that the Three Kings or Magi arrived in Bethlehem bearing gifts for the Child.

December 25 was also the date that an earlier Roman religion, Mithraism, celebrated the birth of the Unconquered Sun on the last day of a week-long holiday for Saturn, the god of agriculture. This was a time of feasting, music, and dancing at the end of one year's harvest and before the preparation for the next growing season. All business was suspended for the week, and only bakers and cooks were working, as feasting was an important part of the holiday. During this time, too, servants and masters sat down together as equals at the feasts.

By the sixth century, Christ's Mass had also become a public holiday. The twelve days from December 25 to January 6 were a holiday season, and some of the old pagan ways still stayed on in the Christian celebration.

In Sicily at Syracuse, a festival is held to honor Saint Lucia on her birthday, December 13, when her silver image is carried in a procession to the cathedral. In some areas great bonfires are lighted from burning straw torches rushed through the streets by men and boys. This day in the old calendar was the shortest day of the year, and this return of light was part of the celebration.

Saint Lucia's name, too, is close to the Latin *lux*, meaning light, and her feast has always been known as the Feast of Light. Saint Lucia celebrations also take place in Central Europe and in Sweden and Denmark, and in the Swedish section you will read more about her.

Christmas Day is a religious one, with a midnight mass and fasting on Christmas Eve, then a Christmas Day feast and the Nativity scene set up.

It is on Epiphany Eve that Befana, an old lady, puts gifts in the children's shoes which have been left out for this purpose. During the early evening there are parades in some areas with small boys blowing horns as they run through the streets. The legend is that long, long ago the Three Kings passed Befana's house on the way to the Christ Child and asked her to join them. She was cleaning her house and she told them she was too busy. Later in the evening she regretted not going with the Three Kings and rushed down the road after them carrying gifts for the Child, but she could not catch up with their camels. And so, through the centuries on Epiphany Eve (Befana is somehow a shortening of Epiphania), she has rushed around with presents, leaving them at all houses with children.

NATIVITY SCENE FIGURES (*Presèpio*)

Christmas in Italy is mainly a religious holiday with the celebration centered around the Nativity scenes in church and home. Saint Francis of Assisi created the first scene in Greccio, and in his church in Assisi there is a painting by Giotto showing the scene. The clay figures are sold in markets, the largest being in Rome at the Piazza Navona and in Naples. In Naples, families create large scenes with cardboard mountains, caves, buildings, rivers of crushed glass, all covered with moss, and all the figures of Mary, Joseph, the baby resting on straw, shepherds, animals, and angels hung overhead. The Three Kings slowly arrive at the center scene during the days from Christmas to January 6, Three Kings' Day. There is a large public Nativity scene in Naples that is famous for its beauty and elaborate staging, and people come from all over to see it.

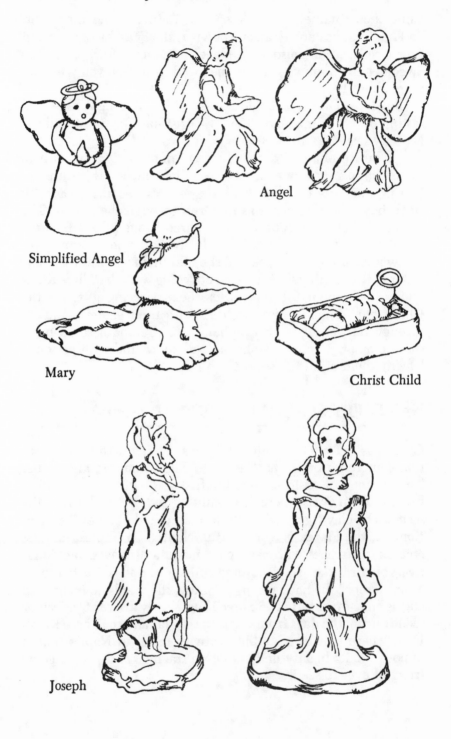

Angel

Simplified Angel

Mary

Christ Child

Joseph

In this project the figures are made of clay, either oven-baked or air-dried, and covered first with acrylic polymer gloss medium, then with white acrylic paint. You are on your own in modeling the figures, so follow the drawings that suggest some of the forms your figures may take. This is the way a true craftsperson works.

Materials and Tools
clay, oven-baked or air-dried, 2- to 5-pound box
tools for working with clay
acrylic polymer gloss medium
acrylic paint, white
ruler
flat nylon brush, ½ inch wide
small container for mixing paint

Directions
1. First read all the directions on handling clay in the last chapter.
2. Look carefully at the drawings as basic designs, then follow them in your own way. Be sure to hollow out the standing figures after they are made so they will dry evenly. Check all bottoms of figures so that they will stand evenly on a flat surface.
3. Let the figures dry very well. Bake the oven-baked clay according to directions; the air-dried clay will be ready for the next step once it is thoroughly dry and hard. The oven-baked clay will be ready for painting as soon as it has been baked.
4. Cover all surfaces, including the hollowed-out centers, with acrylic polymer gloss medium. Let dry, then add a second coat and let dry well.
5. Mix white paint with a little gloss medium to thin out the paint so it can be brushed on the figures. Cover all the outside surfaces with the white paint. Let dry and add a second coat so the covering is pure white. Let dry.
6. Arrange figures in a Nativity scene, called a *presèpio* by the Italians, adding any small farm animals you may have, perhaps the Woolly Sheep if you have made one (page 54). You can make more figures, such as angels, shepherds, or Three Wise Men, and even try your hand at farm animals. And hang a star up over everything.

Scandinavia

✤ ✤ ✤

The half-remembered pagan rites of farmers concerned for their livestock and harvests have been incorporated into the Christian celebrations of the month-long Christmas season. These celebrations are very similar in Denmark, Finland, Norway, and Sweden where in December the sun sets at three o'clock in the afternoon (or even earlier in the northernmost areas) and the long northern night sets in. The sun is sorely missed as the winter solstice nears on December 20 and hope for the return of the sun grows strong. All longing for the sun and symbols of the warm south become part of Christmas; citrus fruits, spices such as cardamom, saffron, and turmeric, and candles to light the darkness.

These candles were thick and could burn all night on Christmas Eve until church service on Christmas Day. Many superstitions were connected with the length of time a candle or several candles burned and which one went out first, superstitions connected with good harvests or foretelling death or misfortunes. Because of the long darkness and stormy weather, all sorts of trolls or old pagan gods were abroad before cockcrow on Christmas day so that it was wise to stay indoors at that time.

Norway has its mischievous *Julenisse* gnomes, who play tricks on the farmers and the farm animals, and Father Frost is a standard part of the Christmas season. The actual Christian Christmas was established in Norway in the middle of the tenth century.

Sweden's holiday season begins with Saint Lucia Day on December 13, which is the birthday of Sicily's Saint Lucia, but is also the shortest day of the year by Sweden's old calendar. The Saint Lucia song sung at this time is set to the old Neapolitan tune *Santa Lucia*. This inclusion of Saint Lucia in a Swedish celebration may have been brought back from Sicily by the Crusaders who occupied Sicily for so many years. The Latin word *luci* is the singular of *lux*, meaning light, and *lucifer* (bringer of light) is another word for the planet Venus, the brilliant morning star which is often thought of as the Christmas star. It is fun to speculate on transference of customs from one country to another and how it came about.

"Santa Claus" in Swedish is *Jultomten*; *Jule* is Yule and *tomten* is a sort of playful household god, never seen, who moved things around in the house, upset milk buckets, and tucked things away in odd places. Early in the celebration of Christmas, disguised givers tossed their presents in the front door of friends, then quickly disappeared. This custom gradually developed into the *Jultomten* as the giver of gifts.

Twelfth Night was also celebrated by groups of young people parading in the villages, following three of their members dressed as the Three Kings. They carried a large six-pointed star, and sang special songs, which is a custom found in other parts of northern Europe.

WOODEN CUTOUTS FOR THE TREE
(*Rosemaling*)

Norwegian tree decorations are called *rosemaling* and by tradition are made of thin wood boards cut into shapes, then painted and decorated in bright colors. Shapes include bells, trees, birds, houses, angels, people, and many more designs. These are kept from year to year and freshened with new paint whenever needed.

This project uses flat boards of balsa wood and small cans and craft bottles of enamel for the bright decorations.

Materials and Tools
typewriter paper
balsa wood, ¼ × 6 × 36 inches
facial tissues
white shellac, 8-ounce can
enamel, 8-ounce cans, red, green
enamel, ¾- to 1-ounce bottles, white, yellow, light blue
sandpaper
string
pencil
ruler
scissors
craft knife
craft saw
wood file
hand drill or thin nail
flat watercolor brush, ¾ inch wide
round watercolor brush, #2

Directions

1. Before beginning this project read the sections on Working with Wood and Painting in the last chapter.

2. Enlarge the patterns on the typewriter paper by the grid method. Cut out patterns and place on the balsa wood strip. Trace around the edges with a pencil. Cut out the shapes with either the craft knife or saw or both, depending on the shape.

Step 1

Enlarge all squares to ½″

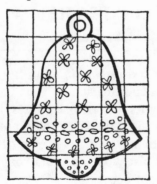
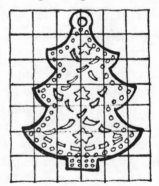

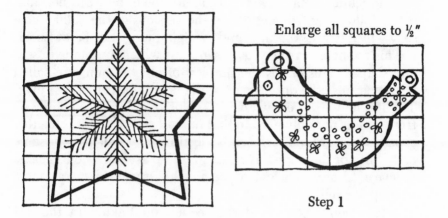

Enlarge all squares to ½″

Step 1

3. Smooth all edges with the file, then sandpaper all surfaces. Dust off with facial tissues.

4. Cover all surfaces with shellac, using the flat watercolor brush.

5. When the shellac has dried, cover all sides of the wood with enamel paint, some with red, others with green. When dry, add a second coat and let dry.

6. Decorate both sides of the cutouts with small dots of the other colors, using the round #2 brush and following the designs on the drawings or making your own designs.

7. Drill a hole at the top of each cutout with the hand drill, or use a thin nail to punch out a hole. Run a length of string through the hole and tie the two ends at the top at a length suitable for hanging on a tree branch.

SAINT LUCIA BUNS ("CATS")

In Sweden on the morning of Saint Lucia Day, December 13, the oldest girl in the family, wearing a long white dress and a circlet of lighted candles on her head, carries a breakfast tray with coffee and Saint Lucia buns to her parents' bedroom. Brothers and sisters follow her, singing one of the versions of the Saint Lucia song which stresses darkness and the light brought by Saint Lucia.

This recipe is for the yeast-risen buns which are made in several shapes. This one is the simplest of all; the buns are called "cats" because the double curl of the dough looks like cat's eyes. Traditionally, the yellow dough is colored and flavored with saffron. This is not only hard to find in most stores, but it is terribly expensive, so ground turmeric is substituted. It will give the same color but not the same flavor, and is often used in Swedish cakes to give a yellow, eggy look to the dough. Or you can use a couple of drops of yellow food coloring.

Before you begin, read the section on Baking in the last chapter.

CAUTION: Never use sharp kitchen equipment or the stove or oven without asking a responsible adult to help you.

Ingredients
This will make 9 to 12 buns.
> 1 tablespoon dry yeast
> 2 tablespoons lukewarm water
> 4 tablespoons butter
> 6 tablespoons milk
> 4 tablespoons sugar
> 2 eggs (1 egg for dough, 1 for brushing on
>   dough before baking)
> ⅛ teaspoon salt
> 2 cups all-purpose flour
> ⅛ to ¼ teaspoon ground turmeric (optional)
> 4 tablespoons raisins
> 18 to 24 whole raisins

Directions
1. Put lukewarm water (just warmer than body temperature) in a small bowl and sprinkle yeast over the surface. Place in a warm area until yeast is foamy.
2. Cut the 4 tablespoons of raisins in half and set aside.
3. Melt butter in a small saucepan over low heat. When

melted, take off the heat, add the milk, and let cool to luke-warm. Pour into a mixing bowl.

4. Add one egg and beat with a table fork. Slowly add the sugar and mix with a metal or wooden tablespoon. Add the foamy yeast and mix well.

5. Place 1½ cups of flour in the sifter and add salt and ⅛ teaspoon turmeric. Gradually sift flour over the liquid in the bowl, mixing well before adding more flour. When all the flour is incorporated, add the chopped raisins.

6. Set the remaining ½ cup of flour aside. Dust a small amount of this flour over the top of the dough. Cover the top of the bowl with a dish towel. Put bowl in a warm place and let dough rise for one hour.

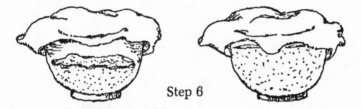

Step 6

7. Punch down the dough and add ¼ cup of the flour to the dough, stirring it in with a spoon. (If dough does not seem yellow enough, add the other ⅛ teaspoon of turmeric to this ¼ cup of flour before adding flour to the dough.)

8. Flour the pastry board with some of the remaining ¼ cup of flour. Scrape dough onto board, folding and punching it into a flat, rectangular shape. Add the rest of the flour if dough is sticky.

9. Roll the dough to a ¾-inch thickness, one side measuring 8 inches. Cut into 8-inch long strips. Make a note of the width you cut so that if you want to make a change the next time you make

Step 9

Saint Lucia buns, you will know the original measurement. Curl strips around into double rounds (see drawing) and place a whole raisin in the center of each round.

10. Put buns on a greased baking sheet, allowing space for rising between them. Cover with a towel and let rise for 30 minutes in a warm place. Ten or fifteen minutes before the buns are ready, turn the oven on to 450° F.

11. Remove towel from pan and brush tops of buns with beaten egg to which 1 teaspoon of water has been added. Place in oven and bake for 10 to 12 minutes. Take out and transfer to a baking rack and let cool. The buns can be reheated slightly before serving.

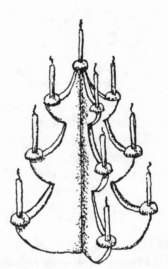

WOODEN CANDLE-TREE

Green trees and candles are symbols of the northern Christmas. Evergreens are the promise that green will come again to the bare tree branches and white landscape. Candles are the promise that the sun will return to chase away the long, dark winter nights that start at three o'clock in the afternoon.

A candlestick made of wood in the shape of a green Christmas tree has round candleholders at the ends of the branches. These trees are part of a family's Christmas traditions in Sweden, brought out each year so the flames of red or white candles can flicker in the center of the table to light the evening meal.

If you do not want to use candles, cut short lengths of wooden dowel and paint them with red or white paint.

Materials and Tools
typewriter paper
carbon paper
balsa wood, ¼ × 6 × 16 inches
sandpaper
salt dough, ¼ recipe (see page 165)
plastic bag
13 birthday cake size candles, ⁹⁄₁₆ × 2 inches,
　　red or white
contact cement
shellac, small can
flat paint, small cans of green and red
pencil
ruler
scissors
craft saw
craft knife
file
flat watercolor brush, ¾ inch wide
round watercolor brush, #5

Variation:
illustration board, 6 × 16 inches
wooden dowel, ¼ × 26 inches
acrylic or poster paint, green
flat nylon brush, ¾ inch wide

Directions
　　1. Enlarge the pattern by the grid method on a sheet of typewriter paper. Cut out around the outline.

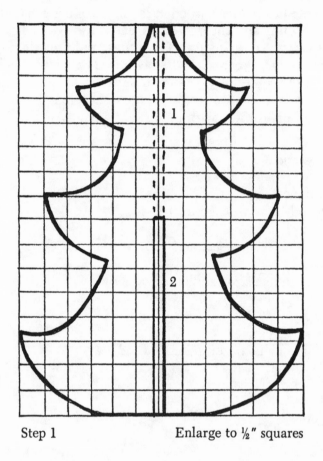

Step 1   Enlarge to ½" squares

2. Lay the pattern on one end of the balsa-wood board and draw around the outline. Slip a piece of carbon paper under the pattern, and with a ruler and pencil outline the top slot, labeled 1. Repeat the outlining of the pattern on the other half of the board, and add the bottom slot, labeled 2.

3. With the craft saw or knife, cut out both trees around the edges, then cut out the two slots. Put the two trees together with the slots so they are at right angles to each other. The bottoms of both trees should rest firmly on a flat surface. If not, correct any unevenness by filing away a little wood either at the end or top of one slot, or from the bottom of the trees.

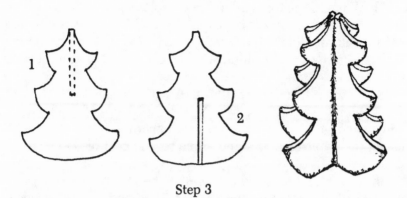

Step 3

4. File and sandpaper all edges and flat surfaces until smooth. Set aside until the individual candleholders are made, so all shellacking and painting can be done at the same time.

5. To make the candleholders, make one-quarter of the recipe for Salt Dough in the last chapter.

6. Scoop out 13 level teaspoonfuls of salt dough and put them into a plastic bag so they will stay moist until you finish forming the candleholders. Roll one piece into a small ball with the palms of your hands. Flatten ball a bit, and curve up around the end of a candle so it is held firmly within the ball. Flatten the bottom of the holder, then make a slot with the craft knife ¼ inch wide and ⅛ inch deep, the length of the center bottom. Put the holder over the flat end of a branch to make sure that the slot fits over the wood. Remember that the salt dough will shrink as it dries, so make the slot just a little wider than the wood. Put holder to one side to dry. Make the twelve other holders. You may not need a full teaspoon for each candleholder.

Step 6

7. When the candleholders are completely dry, check the size of the openings by placing a candle in each one. If the opening has shrunk too much, scrap away some of the hardened dough with the craft knife or sandpaper. Also check each bottom slot for fit.

8. Cover all surfaces of the tree with shellac using the flat watercolor brush. Then cover the sides and tops of the holders, let dry and shellac the bottoms. Sandpaper the first coat of shellac on the two tree pieces and add a second coat of shellac to all sides.

9. Cover all the wood surfaces of the tree with green paint using the flat watercolor brush. Let dry, sandpaper if needed, then add a second coat of green.

10. When shellac is dry on the candleholders, cover them with red paint, using the #5 watercolor brush. When dry, add a second coat of paint and let dry.

11. Place the two halves of the tree together with the slots so they are at right angles to each other. Attach the candleholders with contact cement (see Gluing and Cementing in last chapter). Spread contact cement in the bottom groove of each candleholder. Spread contact cement on the matching surface width at the flat end of each branch. Let contact cement dry. When dry, press holders into place at the end of each branch.

12. Ask an adult to quickly melt a spot at the end of a candle, then press into holder before wax hardens. Repeat with each candle. Birthday candles will burn for only a short time.

Variation: Use illustration board instead of balsa wood, following Steps 1–3. Paint board with either acrylic or poster paint, using the flat nylon brush for the acrylic paint, and the flat watercolor brush for the poster paint.

Substitute painted wooden dowels for the candles. Saw the ¼ inch in diameter wooden dowel into thirteen 2-inch-long pieces. Whittle one end of each piece into a point, using the craft knife. Shellac surfaces, let dry, then paint with flat red paint, using the round #5 watercolor brush. Dry between each coat. When dry, fasten to candleholders with contact cement. You can also use wooden dowel "candles" on the balsa-wood tree.

WHEAT WREATH

At Christmastime in Sweden the houses are decorated with braided wreaths made of long straws from the last sheaf of the wheat or rye harvest. Two small bunches of grain ears are crossed at the bottom of the wreath and held in place with red ribbon or tape tied in a bow. This means good luck to the house and a good harvest for the next year, a custom left over from pagan days.

Unless you live near or on a farm, or have a craft shop nearby that sells wheat straw for weaving, you will have to use raffia for the braided wreath. The grain ears are often sold in florist shops or garden centers in the section of dried flowers, seed pods, and dried leaves.

Materials and Tools
typewriter paper
self-sticking tape, clear
raffia, 1-pound package, natural color
wheat ears, 20 to 24 (or fewer), 4 to 6 inches long
picture hanging wire, one package
ribbon or tape, ½ × 24 inches, red
button and carpet thread, tan
pencil
ruler
scissors
compass
wire clippers

Directions
1. Put two sheets of typewriter paper together to form a sheet 11 × 16 inches. With a compass, draw a circle 9¼ inches in diameter in the center of the paper. If you do not have a compass this large, then make your own. Tie one end of button and carpet thread 1 inch above the pencil point. Make a mark on the thread 4½ inches from the knot. Put a pencil dot in the center of the paper. Hold the mark on the thread over the dot with thumb and forefinger of one hand; with the other hand hold the pencil upright, point touching the paper. Draw a circle on the paper, keeping the thread taut and the pencil upright. Do not move the marked spot away from the center pencil dot.

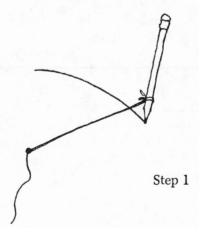

Step 1

2. Form raffia fibers into three separate strands, each one rolled into a loose rope a little less than 1 inch wide. Hold the three ropes together with wire wrapped around one end. Braid the three strands together (see Appalachian Wreath, page 123, for directions). The strands of fibers forming the wreath are 1 yard long. You may have to keep adding raffia to the strands to make this length. Tuck in the ends before you run out of length and roll the existing fibers around the new ones.

3. As you braid the raffia, check the size of the wreath against the 9¼-inch circle to see how much more raffia will be needed. The braided area should be 1¾ to 2 inches wide. When the right length is reached, overlap the two ends 1½ inches, and hold together with the wire wrapped around the wreath several times, the ends twisted together. Cut off wire with wire clippers and tuck ends into wreath.

4. Gather the wheat-ear stems into two bunches, and tie each one with button and carpet thread 1¼ inches from the ends.

5. Place the two bunches over the joining of the wreath ends, crossing the stems over each other, ends below the wreath, seed heads inside the wreath. Tie bunches in place with the red ribbon or tape. Make a wide bow on top of the holding knot.

6. Tie a loop of button and carpet thread at the center top of the wreath between the fibers, knotting the ends for a hanging loop.

Variation: If you can find wheat straw, soak it in water before using it; braid it and form it into a circle while it is still soft and wet. Let dry before adding wheat heads and ribbon.

Thailand

‡ ‡ ‡

In Thailand where the religion is Buddhism, a few people celebrate Christmas, and there are Christmas religious services at the
French missions and schools. Some department stores are decorated for Christmas American-style and display gifts.

Thai crafts are made mostly of woven straw as baskets, trays,
hats, place mats, or brightly colored flat fish and animals to hang
as decorations. The hand-woven and dyed silks are used for
clothes, wall hangings, and cushions.

STRAW FISH

This project is a Thai design of a woven straw fish with a "hidden" opening the length of the side. The fish is a Christian symbol from ancient times and can be hung on a wall with Christmas

cards tucked into the opening. Made from a finely woven straw place mat, each section is stained with different colors, the edges bound with colored plastic tape.

Materials and Tools
typewriter paper
woven-straw place mat, 12 × 18 inches
self-sticking tape, ½ inch wide, clear
self-sticking tape, ⅜ or ½ inch wide, red,
    deep yellow, green
fabric, 12¾ × 17½ inches (approximately,
    see Step 6), red
acrylic paints or colored inks, purple, magenta red,
    medium green, chrome yellow
paper towels
felt-tipped pen, black
contact cement
string
pencil
ruler
scissors
pins
flat nylon brush, ¾ inch wide
small containers for mixing paint

Directions
1. Put four sheets of typewriter paper together with clear self-sticking tape to form a sheet 16 × 21 inches. Enlarge the pattern (see next page) by the grid method on the typewriter paper. Cut out the separate pieces of the pattern.
2. Lay pattern on the place mat, being sure that the straight lines on each piece follow horizontal weaving lines on the mat. Hold patterns in place with small pieces of clear tape. Cut out the separate pieces, cutting through the clear tape.
3. Color the upper surfaces of the straw shapes with either inks or acrylic paint thinned out with water. Do not soak pieces with liquid as it is better to put on two light coats or more, with drying time in between. If straw starts to curl, put paper towels

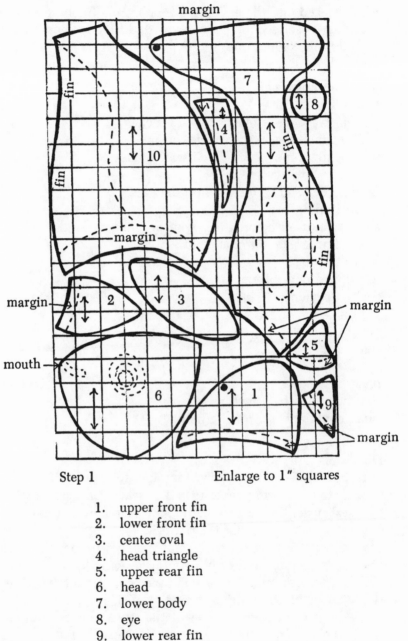

Step 1   Enlarge to 1″ squares

1. upper front fin
2. lower front fin
3. center oval
4. head triangle
5. upper rear fin
6. head
7. lower body
8. eye
9. lower rear fin
10. main body

• – front fin
• – top of tail } glue hanging loop, Step 7

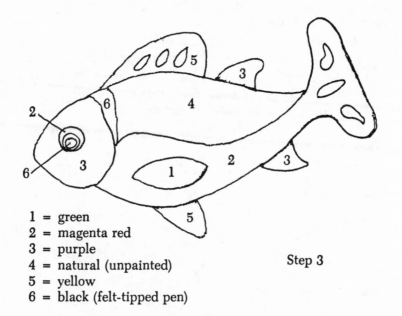

1 = green
2 = magenta red
3 = purple
4 = natural (unpainted)
5 = yellow
6 = black (felt-tipped pen)

Step 3

over the straw and then a heavy book on top, such as a telephone book.

4. Bind edges with tape. First bind the outer two sides of the two front fins, the center oval, and the right side of the head triangle (piece #4) with yellow tape. The upper rear fin, the back of the head, and the top edge of the lower body are bound with red tape. The round eye and the lower rear fin are bound with green tape.

5. The next step is to put the pieces together with contact cement (see Gluing in the last chapter for directions).

a. Spread contact cement on underside of the small head triangle and on the matching upper surface of the natural color

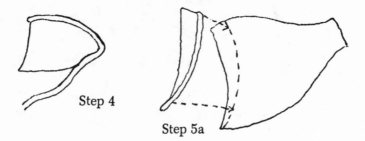

Step 4

Step 5a

main body of the fish along the front curve. Let dry, then press the two surfaces together.

b. Spread a ¼ inch wide line of contact cement on the bottom edge and front curve of the underside of the red half-fish. Add a matching ¼ inch wide line of contact cement along the lower facing edge of the natural-color body of the fish and along the front curve over the triangle. Let dry, then put the two pieces together. You now have a pocket between the full body of the fish and the red lower half.

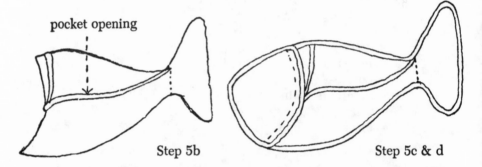

Step 5b   Step 5c & d

c. Spread a ⅜ inch wide line of contact cement along the underside of the back edge of the head. Add a matching line along the front curve of the body, on part of the triangle and front of the red lower half along the margins. Let dry and press together.

d. Edge the top and bottom of the head, the natural color body top edge, the tail, and the bottom of the red lower half of the fish with the green tape.

e. Add a ½ inch wide line of contact cement to the bottom edges of the margins (the untaped sides) of all four fins on the

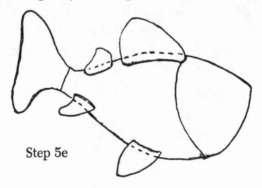

Step 5e

right sides. Turn the fish to the wrong side and add matching ¼ inch strips of contact cement on the back of the fish, checking the patterns for placement. When cement is dry, put fins in place.

f. Add a ¼ inch wide line of contact cement around the back edge of the eye and the oval decoration. Press lightly in position so some of the cement is transferred to the fish. Then add more cement to the transferred line as well as adding to the eye and oval edges. Let dry and press into place.

g. Cut out two circles from the white typewriter paper to match the two inner eye circles on the pattern. Cover the smallest circle with black, using the felt-tipped pen. Cover back of larger white circle with contact cement and also add a matching circle of cement to the straw eye circle. Let dry and press into position. Repeat with the black circle which is cemented to the white circle.

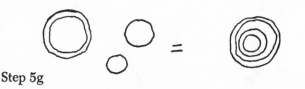

Step 5g

h. Add mouth with yellow tape.

i. Cut three "leaf" patterns from the red tape, and three "leaf" patterns from the green tape (your choice of size and shape), and press into position: the red on the upper front fin, the green on the tail.

Step 5i

6. Next make the pattern for the red cloth backing. Put four pieces of typewriter paper together with clear self-sticking tape so that you have a sheet slightly larger than the fish. Turn the fish face down on the paper and trace around the edge with a lead pencil. Add a ¼-inch margin all around the edge and cut out the pattern. Pin to the red fabric and cut out. Remove pins and pattern and turn in the ¼-inch margin, pressing a crease with your fingers along the fold line.

7. Spread a ¼ inch wide line of contact cement all around the edge of the fish on the wrong side. Add contact cement to the margin of the red cloth. Make two 3-inch-long loops with the string and place in position on front fin and tail; 1 inch of the string ends is smoothed inside the top line of the fin and tail. Add extra contact cement over the string ends and on the matching line inside the red cloth. Let cement dry, then smooth red cloth backing into place.

8. Hang up the fish and tuck Christmas cards in the pocket. After Christmas is over, hang the fish in your room as a secret hiding place, or tuck reminder notes to yourself in the pocket.

China

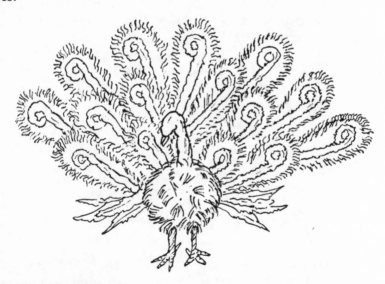

While most Chinese do not celebrate Christmas, small Christmas tree decorations are made and sent to other countries: angels, peacocks, strings of little embroidered-satin diamond and heart shapes.

PROUD PEACOCK

In this project the small peacock is made of bright-colored feathers and chenille stems and balls (available in variety stores).

Materials and Tools
typewriter paper
15 feathers, medium tip plumes, 3 inches long,
    moss green
10 feathers, 3 inches long, orange
chenille stems, 1 package, light green
chenille balls, 1 package, bright blue
braided wire picture cord
self-sticking tape, bright blue
white household glue
pencil
ruler
scissors
wire clippers

Directions

1. Measure and draw a 3 × 5 inch rectangle on the typewriter paper. This is the guide for the peacock's spread tail.

2. Cut seven 3½-inch lengths of chenille stems, and nine 3-inch lengths, using the wire clippers or scissors. Curl one end of each stem into a ⅜-inch diameter circle.

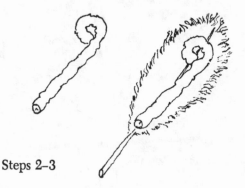

Steps 2–3

3. With the white glue, attach a stem in the center of each green feather, the top of the circle ¼ inch from the upper end of the feather. Repeat until all green feathers are finished and let the glue dry.

4. When dry, make a fan of three rows of feathers, the upper seven having the longest chenille stems. Trim the bottom of the

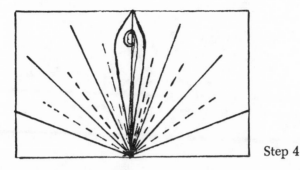

Step 4

rest of the feathers so the next row of six feathers is shorter, and the lower row of two feathers is the shortest of all (about 2 inches).

5. Hold the lower ends of the feathers together with white household glue, leaving the fan undisturbed until dry. When the glue is dry, add eight orange feathers at the base of the fan, four feathers on each side, and attach to the base of the other feathers with the white glue. Let glue dry.

6. Wrap the feather quills together with picture wire into a thick end 1½ inches long, then wrap the wire with the bright blue tape leaving ⅜ inch unwrapped at the end. Bend the top of the end backwards ¼ inch at right angles to the fan. Then bring the rest of the thick end forward. Hold the back end together with more tape.

Step 6

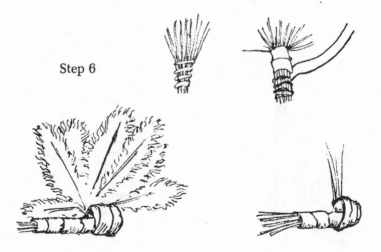

Step 7

7. Cut one chenille ball in quarters. Glue one quarter section to the other ball, separating the fibers to reach the center for gluing. This is the body of the bird. Set aside.

8. For the legs, cut a 4-inch length of picture wire. Unravel ¾ inch at each end; there should be eight separate strands. Divide into four sets of two strands each. Twist each pair of strands together. Wrap blue tape around the length of wire, and around each separate twist of wire. Curve wire into a U shape, the two sides a little more than ¼ inch apart. For the feet, bend three strands forward and one strand backward on each end of the legs. Fasten the ⅜-inch end of wire that is attached to the feather fan (see Step 6) to the top of the U. Wrap with tape so the joining is secure and tight. Glue some small sections of the chenille ball material (from one of the three ¼ pieces left over) to the top of the legs and across the top of the U. About ⅝ inch of the legs is left uncovered.

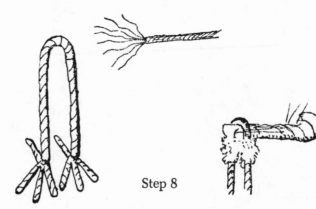

Step 8

9. For the head and neck, cut a 3¼-inch length of chenille stem and two 2¼-inch lengths. Starting ⅜ inch in from one end, wrap the two short pieces of stem around the longer one. Bend the single stem over at the other end so that ½ inch is at right angles to the neck; this is the head of the peacock. Wrap the other end around the joining of legs and tail piece, holding in place with tape.

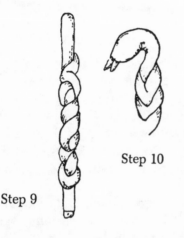

Step 10

Step 9

10. Cut small snippets from the extra orange feathers, gluing two pieces to the end of the head as a beak, and the other pieces in the center of the circles on the tail.

11. Glue the chenille-ball body to the end of the neck, the top of the legs, and the tail wire, right back to the feather fan. If you need a slightly fuller body in front or below the wire joinings, then glue on one or two of the remaining quarters of chenille ball material.

12. For a tree decoration, fasten the feet to the upper side of a tree branch, using a single strand of the picture wire.

The Philippines

❖ ❖ ❖

Christmas in the Philippines is a twenty-two day celebration of feasting and gift giving, parades, singing, and church going, at a time when the mornings are chilly from the northeast monsoon and the rice harvest is in. The long celebration is a mixture of old tribal customs, Chinese, Spanish, European, and American.

On December 16, to start the holiday season, firecrackers and bamboo cannons, introduced centuries ago, are set off early in the morning.

Then comes the midnight mass at churches and cathedrals, a Christmas Eve into Christmas Day custom begun in the early seventeenth century. It is called the Mass of the Cocks, as the cocks begin to crow after midnight. When the story of the birth of Christ is read from the gospel, a star in the choirloft slides down a wire to come to rest above the church's Nativity scene.

When the service is over, everyone spreads out across the square where stalls are set up to sell coffee, tea, and fruit drinks, plus the traditional sticky mixture of flavored and steamed rice called *puto bumbong*. Then home for the Christmas day of visiting and gift giving by friends and relatives.

Parties and gift giving are all part of the next twelve days until Three Kings' Day on January 6.

The *parol* or Christmas star is *the* Christmas custom of the Philippine Islands, appearing throughout the season; it is hung in the window over the Nativity scene in all the homes; the elaborate ones are carried in the Christmas Eve "Parade of the Stars" when all the villages compete for prizes. The large stars are carried in the parade by several people or placed on decorated trucks. Many have a large ring around the outside called a *rolyo* made of newspaper covered with fringes of crepe paper or rice paper. Inside the double star are electric lights or lanterns. The accompanying marchers carry smaller stars.

Generations of *parol*-makers have made the star-lanterns. Whole families are involved, and for some this has grown into a business. Starting in July the men and boys cut the thin stalks of bamboo and make the frames. By October frames of many sizes and shapes have been completed, so the women cut out the covering paper, and all the children help them in pasting the paper to the frames. The stars are trimmed with lace-paper doilies, foil cutouts, tassels and pompoms of fringed paper.

By the middle of November all the stars are ready for sale. Families put up stalls in front of their homes, or rent a shop in town. Some streets are lined with shops one after another selling stars which are closely hung over the sidewalks, the tassels just clearing the heads of passersby. They sell out quickly, and by the middle of December all the stars have been sold.

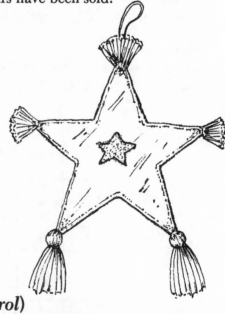

CHRISTMAS STAR (*Parol*)

This is a single star, its bamboo or wooden dowel sticks covered with bright-colored tissue paper and decorated with tissue-paper tassels.

Materials and Tools
typewriter paper
newspaper
bamboo plant supports or wooden dowels, 5
¼ × 36 inches
tissue paper, three 20 × 26-inch pieces, your
choice of color
thin string or button and carpet thread
foil gift-wrap paper
white household glue
thin wire, two 6-inch lengths
pencil
ruler
scissors
felt-tipped pen, black
craft saw
round watercolor brush, #5
small container for mixing glue

Directions

1. Enlarge star pattern by the grid method on a sheet of newspaper, using the felt-tipped black pen.

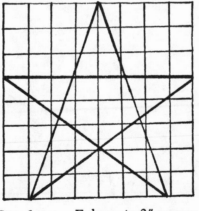

Step 1   Enlarge to 2″ squares

2. For the frame of the star you can use either the green-painted bamboo plant supports sold at garden centers, or the same-size round wooden dowels. Cut the five bamboo or dowel sticks into 20-inch lengths with the craft saw.

3. Lay the five sticks in place on the newspaper pattern, covering the star lines. Tie the ends of the sticks together at the five points with the string or heavy thread, wrapping it around the ends several times before tying a knot. On the top point, after tying the knot, form a 6-inch-long loop for hanging the star, then tie the loop in place at the end of the point. Also tie together the five inner crossing points. Soak all the string at each point with glue and let dry completely.

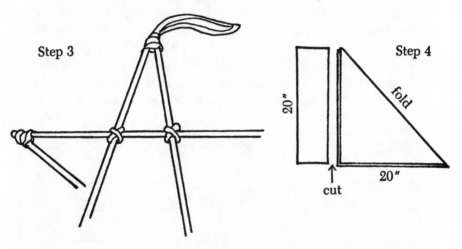

Step 3

Step 4

20"

fold

cut   20"

4. Fold a 20 × 26-inch sheet of tissue paper to make a square. Cut away the extra strip of paper, keeping the strip for the fringes. Repeat with another sheet of tissue paper. Unfold both squares.

5. Transfer star to a clean sheet of newspaper. Cover the top surface of the star with white glue mixed with a little water, using the round brush. If any glue has dropped on the newspaper, carefully pick up the star and transfer it to a clean sheet of newspaper, without touching the glue.

6. Carefully place one square sheet of tissue paper over the star, smoothing it into place. Press gently with a finger along the glued areas. Let dry.

7. With the scissors, carefully trim away excess paper from the five points of the star.

8. Turn the star over, and *very carefully* "paint" the other side of the sticks with a light coat of glue, bringing the glue over the outside edges. Do not drop any glue on the tissue paper! Lay the second square of tissue paper over the glued sticks, smooth it into place, and lightly press it against the glued sticks and over the sides. Let dry thoroughly.

9. While the glue is drying, cut out two foil-paper stars for the center of each side of the large star. Enlarge the star grid squares to ½ inch each on the typewriter paper, then cut out the pattern. Use the pattern to cut two stars from the foil paper.

10. Cut away the extra paper from the large star. Paste foil stars *by the points only* to the center of each side of the large star.

11. To make the paper tassels for the two bottom points, cut two pieces of tissue paper 8 × 16 inches each. Fold the 16-inch length in half. With the scissors, make cuts ⅜ inch wide and 6 inches long, leaving a 2-inch margin at the folded side. Repeat

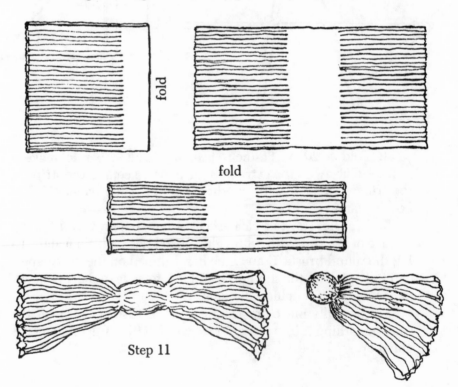

fold

Step 11

with the other sheet of tissue paper. Open up the two sheets so the fringes are on both ends. Then fold one sheet in half lengthwise, and squeeze the plain center into gathers with the fingers. Fold the middle of the center area in half, so all the fringes are together. Wrap one end of a 6-inch length of fine wire around the bottom of the center area just at the top of the fringe. Twist the end of the wire around the longer length so it pinches the paper into a rounded top of the tassel. Push the longer end of the wire up through the center of the tassel and out the top. Repeat with the other length of fringed paper.

12. Attach a tassel to each lower point of the star with the wire.

13. Cut in half the two leftover 6 × 20-inch pieces of tissue paper, discarding one piece and keeping the other three pieces. Fold each piece in half across the 3-inch measure, then in half again. Between the two folded edges, cut the paper into ⅛ × 2-inch fringes, leaving 1 inch uncut. Open up and spread out on a piece of newspaper. Lightly spread glue over the solid, 1 inch wide area. Wrap the glued area around and around itself at the end of one side point of the star. Repeat with the other two strips, attaching one to the other side point, and the third to the top point. Be sure that the hanging loop is free of the fringe and is in place through the center of the puff of fringe.

14. Hang the star in a window.

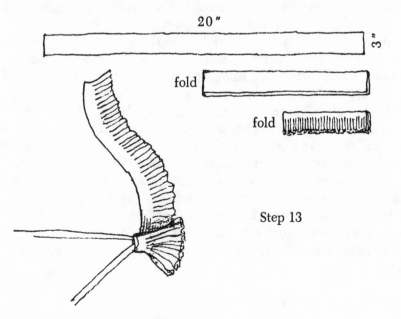

20 "

3 "

fold

fold

Step 13

United States

✤ ✤ ✤

Christmas celebrations in the United States center around Christmas Eve and Christmas Day, with customs varying in different parts of the country reflecting the settlers' home countries: the Dutch in New York; Moravians in Pennsylvania; Swedish in Minnesota and Pennsylvania; English originally in New England and the Eastern coast; Spanish on the West coast; Italians on the East Coast; French in Louisiana; Greeks in Florida—the list could go on and on. Climate and local foods often changed the original celebrations.

In the northeast, Christmas trees were trimmed with strings of popcorn or cranberries, Christmas stockings were hung on the fireplace mantel with a new penny and an orange in the toe. The Puritans in New England followed the edicts of Oliver Cromwell, and passed a law against Christmas celebrations in 1659. While the law was repealed in 1681, habits had been formed so it took a long time to make this a joyous celebration.

New Amsterdam (New York) in the days of the Dutch colony in 1626 celebrated Saint Nicholas Day on December 6. He was called *Sinterklass* at that time, and when the English conquered the Dutch in 1664, they adopted the good saint as a giver of gifts. However his "day" of gift giving gradually changed to December 25, and he became a little heavier. In 1822, Clement Clarke Moore, who lived in New York City on Twenty-third Street near the Hudson River, wrote *'Twas the Night Before Christmas*, about the visit of Saint Nicholas with his gifts. But it was in 1865 that Thomas Nast, a famous cartoonist, drew the Santa Claus with a red suit, white whiskers, and pot belly, thereby setting the style for all the jolly Santas to follow.

In Bethlehem, Pennsylvania, the influence is Moravian. They

had settled in this area, coming from Bohemia (now part of Czechoslovakia) in the early part of the eighteenth century. In 1755 the first Christmas Crib, a *Putze*, was set up in that stockaded town of Bethlehem on Christmas Eve when the Indians planned to attack. But up in the Bell-House Tower, trombones played Christmas music, and the awed and superstitious Indians ran back into the forest as the music floated through the air. And so, in the morning the children saw their Christmas Crib, received apples and bright ribbons, and sang "The Morning Star." And ever since, evergreens are gathered as background for the *Putzes* that are set up in every home, some filling a whole room. A Christmas Love Feast with sugar buns is still served, and the trombones play at Christmas.

In Los Angeles the *Posada* groups trail through the streets of the Mexican section with their lanterns and Nativity figures, as they visit the homes of friends and relatives.

All over the country, families still celebrate with the old customs and in some areas, features from several countries are blended together into a new celebration.

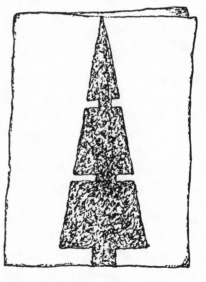

CHRISTMAS CARD

Even though the first Christmas card was printed in England around 1843, it was not until the 1860s that cards became popular in England and in the United States, the first ones being printed in the Boston area. Now they are made and sent all over the world wherever Christmas is celebrated.

It is fun to make your own card, as no one else will have the same kind. Cut a Christmas tree design from a styrofoam block, dab color over the design, press the block on a sheet of paper, and there is your card. You can make many designs and, if you keep your blocks from year to year, you can sometimes print two designs one over the other, using two colors to make an interesting combination.

Materials and Tools
typewriter paper
styrofoam block, 4 × 6 × 1¼ inches
acrylic paint, green, or
    water-based block printing ink, green
sheets of drawing paper, 8 × 6 inches
tools and supplies for block printing with styrofoam
    (see Block Printing in the last chapter)
felt-tipped pen, black
pencil
ruler
scissors

Directions
   1. Read the section on Block Printing in the last chapter for directions on cutting the block, making a dabber, applying the ink, and printing the design on paper. Put a marker in this section and refer to it all through this project.
   2. Enlarge the design by the grid method on the typewriter paper. Cut out the design and lay it on the 4 × 6-inch sytrofoam block. Trace around the edges with the felt-tipped pen, then cut out the design with the craft knife.
   3. Make the dabber and mix acrylic paint with water, or mix water-based block printing ink with water.
   4. Add color to block with dabber, turn block over, and print your first impression. Correct the amount of ink needed, then continue to print on the right half of the 8-inch width of the paper. Keep printing until you have the number of cards you will need. Let cards dry undisturbed in a single layer.

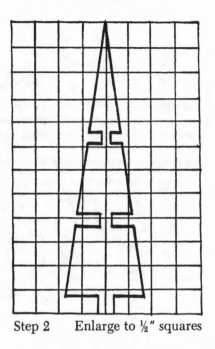

Step 2   Enlarge to ½" squares

5. Fold cards in half, design on the outside, and add a message and your name inside. Put into envelopes, add address and stamp.

6. To mail without an envelope, fold the paper in half with the design inside, and write your message and name on the opposite side. Put name and address and a stamp on the outside. Hold the card together at the bottom with a piece of clear self-sticking tape or a staple.

Step 6

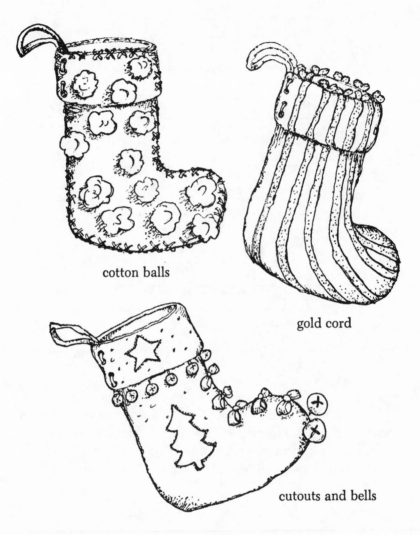

cotton balls

gold cord

cutouts and bells

CHRISTMAS STOCKING

In early Victorian days of nineteenth-century England, hanging stockings from the mantelpiece became a custom. In the United States, particularly in the old Dutch colony of New Amsterdam (later New York when the English took over), stockings were hung up on Saint Nicholas Eve, since wooden shoes were not worn in the new colony. Saint Nicholas was the patron saint of Dutch New Amsterdam.

As both boys and girls wore long, heavy cotton or wool stockings over their knees, there was plenty of length to hold goodies. Since the width stretched, they became long, bumpy objects filled by Saint Nicholas with small mysterious presents, candy, and unshelled nuts. There was always a small new coin in the toe, followed by an orange, the first a symbol of wealth, and the second a symbol of the return of the sun in the coming year.

Home-crafted "stockings" also were made in the shape of Santa Claus's boots. They were cut from bright, sturdy materials, and trimmed with braid or ribbons, decorated with sequins, small Christmas-tree balls or tiny sleigh bells, fabric cutout stars or trees, and even tufts of cotton for snowballs. Each child had his or her own stocking, put away each year to be used again on the following Christmas Eve.

Make the stockings of white or colored felt, trimmed to suit your fancy with whatever you have at hand or decide to buy.

Materials and Tools
typewriter paper
clear self-sticking tape
felt, ¼ yard, or 2 pieces 9 × 12 inches, white,
    red, or green
trimmings; ribbon, braid, sequins, cosmetic cotton puffs
    or absorbent cotton, tiny Christmas tree balls, small
    sleigh bells, fabric cutouts of stars or trees of
    contrasting fabric or felt
button and carpet thread to match or contrast with the felt
white household glue or fabric glue
heavy cord
pencil
ruler
scissors
pins
large-eye needle
flat watercolor brush, ¾ inch wide
small container for mixing glue

Directions

1. The Christmas stocking can be any size, and you can adjust the pattern. The directions in this project are for a small size for a young child and use a standard-size rectangle of felt, 9 × 12 inches. Larger sizes will need more felt.

2. Attach the short sides of two sheets of typewriter paper together with tape. Enlarge the stocking and cuff patterns by the grid method onto this sheet, then cut around the edges.

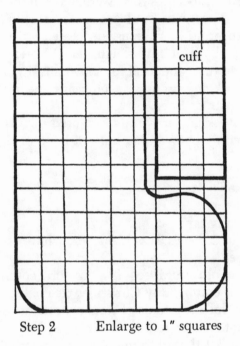

Step 2   Enlarge to 1″ squares

3. Spread the two felt pieces flat on the working surface, right side upright. Pin the patterns to one piece of felt and cut out. Turn the pattern over so the toe is facing in the opposite direction, pin pattern to the felt and cut out.

4. Put the two wrong sides together and sew the two sides and bottom together, leaving the top open. Use a double whipping or overhand stitch. (See Sewing in the last chapter for description and diagram of this stitch.)

5. Sew the two halves of the cuff around the top opening, using the double whipping stitch, then sew the front and back edges of the cuff together with the same stitch.

6. Now that the basic stocking is finished, decorate it in any way you want, or follow one of the illustrations. Ribbon, braid, sequins, fabric cutouts, and cotton puffs are attached with white or fabric glue; Christmas tree balls and sleigh bells are sewn on with thread.

7. To hang up the stocking, make four holes with scissors or paper punch, ½ inch apart through the cuff and stocking, ½ inch from the back seam; repeat on the other side of the seam. Starting from the *inside* of one top hole, put one end of the cord through the hole, then through the next hole to the inside again, out the third hole and back into the fourth hole. Repeat with the other end of the cord through the opposite four holes, again starting at the top. Firmly knot the two ends of the cord, leaving a loop above the cuff for hanging up the stocking. Tack the knot to the inside of the stocking with an overhand stitch.

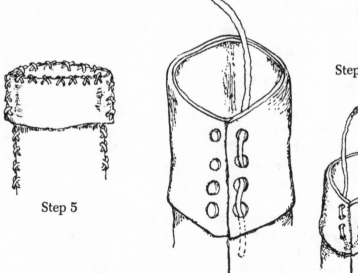

Step 7

Step 5

PUFFED RICE MOLASSES BALLS

Puffed rice balls are an old favorite and easy to make. They are smaller than popcorn balls, and each one can be wrapped in clear food-wrap as holiday gifts, or piled on a plate as a treat for family or visitors. The puffed rice is held together with a molasses syrup, and they melt in the mouth.

CAUTION: Never use sharp kitchen equipment or the stove or oven without asking a responsible adult to help you.

Ingredients
>   4 cups puffed rice
>   ½ cup light corn syrup
>   ½ cup molasses
>   1½ teaspoons cider vinegar
>   ¼ teaspoon salt
>   1 teaspoon vanilla

Directions
   1. Put a large mixing bowl in a 100° F. oven to warm so that the syrup when added to the puffed rice will not harden on the bottom of the bowl.
   2. Combine syrup, molasses, cider vinegar, and salt in a saucepan. Bring to a boil, and cook at a slow boil until the "hard ball" stage is reached—that is, when a few drops of the syrup are dropped into a cup of cold water, they form a hard ball. If you

have a candy thermometer, then cook until the syrup reaches 250° F. Take off heat and add vanilla.

3. Put warmed bowl on the kitchen table and pour in the 4 cups of puffed rice. Slowly add the syrup, stirring the puffed rice with a fork, turning it over and over so all sides are covered with the syrup. If there seems to be too much syrup, add more puffed rice. If syrup starts to cool and thicken in the pan, put it back over the heat to melt.

Step 3

4. With a tablespoon, scoop out enough of the mixture to form a ball about 1½ inches in diameter. Do not squeeze the mixture; the balls should be loosely held together and do not have to be perfectly shaped. You may have to butter your hands to keep the syrup from sticking to them. Work rapidly, and place the balls on a sheet of wax paper as they are formed.

5. Let cool, then wrap each piece in clear plastic food-wrap.

RIBBON CHRISTMAS BALL

Through the years all types of Christmas balls have been made: stuffed cloth, a hard core covered with long strands of colored silk, wool yarn or ribbons, or thin-blown colored glass in all sizes and shapes. The glass balls were bought at Christmastime, and the collection was added to from year to year. The others were handcrafted at home, becoming a part of a family's tradition. They were made from scraps of cloth and trimmings left over from dressmaking, the silk floss from embroidery, and wool yarn from knitting.

Nowadays, a styrofoam ball is the easiest base for this project, as fabric and ribbons can be held in place by just sticking a pin into the ball before the final gluing. This project will be based on one size of styrofoam ball, but you can choose any size and any assortment of ribbons and colors since the possibilities are endless. If each step is followed carefully, you will find that the different-colored ribbons, lace, and braid will be in the right place.

Materials and Tools
styrofoam ball, 3 inches in diameter
trimmings: white and pale yellow velvet ribbon, each 1 × 24
    inches, blue-green satin ribbon 1 × 48 inches, fine gold
    lace ¾ × 48 inches (optional), gold braid ¼ × 48 inches,
    pink satin-covered cord ⅛ × 48 inches, and gold tinsel
    cord 36 inches
fabric glue or white household glue
pencil
ruler
scissors
pins
pearl-headed pin
flat watercolor brush, ¾ inch
    wide
round watercolor brush, #2
small container for mixing glue

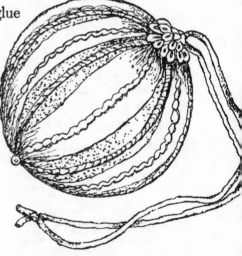

Directions
1. Cut each of the two velvet ribbons into four equal pieces that are 6 inches long. This measurement may be a little long for the 3-inch ball, but it is better to have extra length than too little

material. Cut the satin ribbon into eight equal pieces, each also 6 inches long: the gold braid and lace into eight 6-inch pieces: the pink satin-covered cord into four 12-inch lengths.

2. Find, and mark with a pencil, a top and bottom center on the ball. Starting with one strip of blue satin ribbon, center a pinpoint ¼ inch in from one end, then push the pin into the bottom mark on the styrofoam ball. Stretch ribbon up the side and hold with a pin pushed through the top-center pencil mark on the ball. Cut off excess ribbon to within ¼ inch of the top pin. Repeat with the pieces of blue satin ribbon at equal distances around the ball until all eight pieces are used, lifting the pin as you add each ribbon, and trimming the ends.

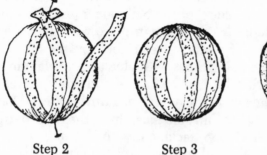

Step 2   Step 3   Step 4

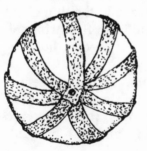

Step 2   blue satin ribbon

3. The next step is to glue the ribbons to the ball. First make a pencil mark on each side of the ribbons on the wide middle of the ball. One by one remove ribbons, tacking each one to the ball with small drops of glue, smoothing them over the ball and matching the pencil marks. Temporarily hold in place with a pin, top and bottom. Let dry.

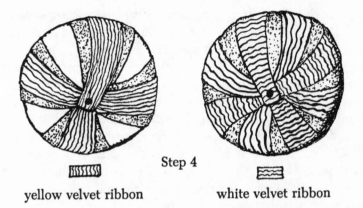

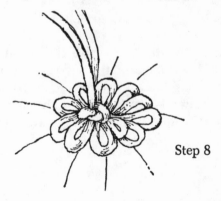

Step 4

yellow velvet ribbon   white velvet ribbon

4. Next add the four pieces of yellow velvet ribbon, spacing them equally on four "sides" of the ball, edges just overlapping the satin ribbon on each side. Tack in place with glue. Repeat with the four pieces of white velvet ribbon on the other four "sides" of the ball, tacking them with glue and overlapping the satin ribbon on each side. Let the yellow and white velvet ribbons dry before going on to the next step. Trim off excess ribbon.

5. If you are using the thin gold lace, this is the time to stretch it over the blue satin ribbon, tacking it with glue *only at the top and bottom* of the ball, and trimming off the extra lace.

6. The next step is to add the thin gold braid at the center of each velvet ribbon, pulling it firmly into place and tacking it top and bottom with glue. If needed, hold in place with pins until the glue dries.

7. Each piece of pink satin cord is centered over the bottom of the ball, then pulled up the center of the blue satin ribbon, the ends meeting at the top. Trim away excess cord and hold the ends in place with glue, and with pins until the glue dries. Stick

Step 8

the long pearl-headed pin into the bottom center of the ball, right through the crossed pink satin cords.

8. Measure off 18 inches of tinsel cord but do not cut it. Make a loop 8 inches long, tying the cord into a knot at the base of this loop. Put glue on the bottom of the knot and pin to the top of the ball. Let dry. The rest of the tinsel cord is glued in place at the top of the ball in a series of small ⅜-inch-long loops that will cover all the ends of the ribbons, braid and cord. Temporarily pin loops in place until glue hardens and dries.

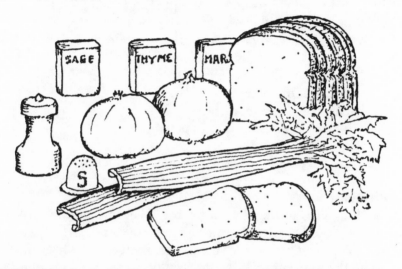

NEW ENGLAND BREAD STUFFING

This is the simplest stuffing of all for turkey or chicken as made by generations of New England cooks. In families, the children always shared in making the stuffing in the warm and busy kitchen. Using materials at hand in the wintertime, it was a tasty and satisfying accompaniment to the holiday roasted bird.

There were always leftover ends of bread, onions in the root cellar, dried sage, lovage, marjoram, and thyme picked from the herb garden in late summer and hung up in the attic to dry. And the turkey or chicken provided the giblets to flavor the stuffing and the broth to moisten the bread. Later on, when celery became available in the winter, it was substituted for the celery-flavored lovage.

The amount of bread depends on the size of the turkey or chicken, but any leftover stuffing can be baked in a covered dish. Ingredients listed will be enough to stuff a 10-pound turkey, and you can adjust the amounts for larger or smaller birds.

CAUTION: Never use sharp kitchen equipment or the stove or oven without asking a responsible adult to help you.

Ingredients

    3 to 4 cups of broken-up dried bread (a solid white bread, thick slices)
    2 onions (each about 2 inches in diameter)
    2 large stalks of celery and leaves
    1 tablespoon dried sage leaves
    1 teaspoon dried thyme
    1 teaspoon dried marjoram
    ½ teaspoon ground black pepper
    salt to taste
    liver, heart, and gizzard of turkey or chicken

Directions

1. Put slices of bread on a baking sheet and place in a 200° oven until slightly dry, but *not* brown and crisp.

2. While the bread is drying in the oven, put the liver, heart, and small pieces cut from the thick outer sides of the gizzard into a small saucepan. Add 2 cups of water, turn on the heat, and bring to a boil; turn down heat when water is boiling and let simmer. Remove liver when done, as it will be cooked before the gizzard pieces. Skim off any foam that rises to the surface of the water. When gizzard and heart are cooked, remove from the liquid. Save the liquid to moisten the stuffing. Cut liver and heart into small pieces.

3. In a large bowl, break bread into pieces, roughly ½ to ¾ inches across. Stir in the giblets with a fork.

4. Peel the onions, slice into ¼-inch-thick slices and cut slices into ¼-inch pieces. Add to bowl and stir with the fork.

5. Wash the celery and shake off the water. Make a cut ⅛ inch from the broad bottom end, and almost through the stalk, then pull back to remove "strings." Cut off leaves, then cut the celery stalks down the center and then cut across in ½-inch slices. Cut up leaves into ½-inch pieces. Add celery and leaves to the bowl. Stir together with fork.

6. Add the seasonings and mix well.

7. Add the giblet water, a few tablespoons at a time, mixing lightly with the fork. Add water until the stuffing is just moist but not soggy; the bread pieces should hold their shape. Taste to see if any more seasonings are needed and correct if they are.

8. If bird is not ready to be roasted, cover bowl with clear plastic-wrap and put in the refrigerator. Do not fill bird until just before it is put into the oven for roasting, as stuffing should not stay inside an uncooked bird. When filling bird, the stuffing should be put in lightly as it will expand in cooking.

APPALACHIAN BRAIDED WREATH

The people who live in the small communities on the sides and in the valleys of the Appalachian Mountains of Virginia, West Virginia, and North Carolina have kept to the old and simple ways of living. Their fabric Christmas wreaths were made from narrow lengths of dress fabric in either solid colors or small patterned materials or a mixture of both, whatever happened to be in Mother's "piece bag." These wreaths were originally stuffed with hay, cotton, wool, or cut-up pieces of fabric. Carefully put away each year, they became part of a family's traditional decorations.

For this wreath the stuffing will be modern polyester fiber filling. Use fabrics with small checks, calico-like, small flowered prints, or plain red, green, and white.

Materials and Tools
fabric, plain or printed cotton or polyester, three pieces
    6 × 42 (or 45) inches
sewing thread to match or blend with fabrics
polyester fiber filling, 16-ounce bag
ribbon, ½ × 36 inches, and ¼ × 8 inches to match
    or contrast with fabric
pencil
ruler
scissors
pins
needle
sewing machine (optional)

Directions
1. Measure and cut three lengths of differently patterned or solid-color fabric, each one measuring 6 × 42 inches. The width of the fabric may be 42 or 45 inches, and you can use either one.

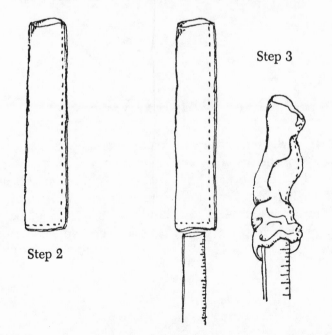

Step 3

Step 2

2. Fold all the pieces in half lengthwise, right sides together. Measure and pin a ½-inch seam on one short end as well as the long side of each piece. Sew up the seams using a reinforced stitch (see Sewing in the last chapter for directions), removing pins as you sew. If you are allowed to use a sewing machine, do so, or have an adult sew the seams for you on the machine.

3. Turn all three tubes inside out, by holding the narrow end of the ruler against the short seam, then pulling the tube back over the ruler. Loosely stuff all three tubes, pushing filling down the length with the ruler. After the tubes have been filled, turn the open edges in to the wrong side and pin. Do not sew them together at this time.

4. Pin the three short seams at the sewn ends of the tubes together for braiding; then test to see if the tubes are filled too loosely or too tightly. Tubes should be stiff enough so the final braided strip will hold a circle shape when the ends are brought together. Unpin the three tubes and correct the filling if needed by adding or taking out some filling, then sew up the three open ends with a blind stitch (see Sewing in the last chapter for directions).

Step 4

Step 5

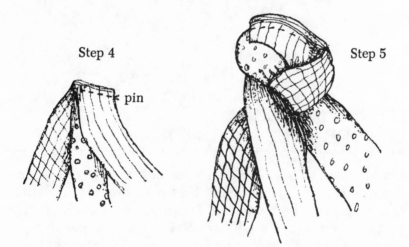

pin

5. Push filling away from ½ inch at one end of each tube, pin tube ends together, and sew the three edges together with a whipstitch (see Sewing in the last chapter for directions). Braid tubes, keeping the long seam underneath, then pin all three to each other at the second end, pushing filling back ½ inch from each end. Sew tubes together with a whipstitch.

6. Curve the braid into a circle, and sew both ends together with a strengthened stitch.

7. Tie the 36-inch ribbon in a bow, and sew the back of the center knot to the seamed ends of the circle.

8. Fold the narrow ribbon in half and sew ends to the center back, on the opposite side of the wreath and level with the bow. This is the hanging loop.

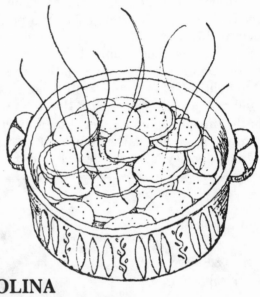

SOUTH CAROLINA ORANGE SWEET POTATOES

In Charleston an old favorite casserole of sweet potatoes or yams is still served at Christmastime. It blended the tropical oranges that came into the markets in December with yams or sweet potatoes from the late fall harvest and brown sugar from the West Indies. Sweet potatoes are light yellow in color with firm flesh, yams are a deep orange in color and the flesh is softer, and either one can be used.

CAUTION: Never use sharp kitchen equipment or the stove or oven without asking a responsible adult to help you.

Ingredients

This recipe will serve 5 or 6 people, using a 2-quart, ovenproof casserole dish.

5 or 6 sweet potatoes or yams, depending on size
1 orange
½ cup dark brown sugar
4 tablespoons butter or margarine (½ stick)

Directions

1. Wash off the sweet potatoes or yams, place in a saucepan, and cover with water. Bring water to a boil, then turn down heat to a gentle boil, and cook until potatoes are just done when tested with a fork (approximately half an hour).

2. Remove from the heat, pour out the hot water, and cool potatoes by running cold water over them while still in the pot. Take out of the pot and remove skins by peeling with a small knife. Cut into ¼-inch-wide slices and pile on a plate.

3. Butter a 2-quart, ovenproof casserole dish.

4. Slice orange as thin as you can. (You may need help from an adult for this). Remove seeds if there are any.

5. Cut butter or margarine into ¼-inch-wide slices, and cut each slice into four pieces. Measure dark brown sugar into a cup. Turn on the oven and set it for 350°.

6. Now you are ready to put the casserole together. Put a layer of sweet potato or yam slices on the bottom of the dish. Add three slices of orange on top of the potato, sprinkle with brown sugar and dot with butter. Cover with potato slices, then orange, brown sugar and butter, and continue layering the ingredients, ending up with potato over the top. Sprinkle top with sugar and dot with butter. If you have run out of sugar and butter, add more.

7. Add water to the casserole, pouring it from a cup down the side so as not to disturb the sugar between the layers. Water should fill the dish halfway to the top layer.

8. Put in the oven and bake 30 to 45 minutes, until orange rind is soft and juice has thickened. Take out of the oven and serve hot. This can be cooked earlier in the day and reheated at dinner time

AMBROSIA

In Georgia, South Carolina, and Florida as well as along the Gulf Coast, Christmas weather can be warm so ambrosia is a favorite Christmas dinner dessert. In the early days it was a rare treat as bananas and coconuts had to travel from the Caribbean Islands by sailing ships, and the overland transportation of oranges was slow too.

This is an easy-to-make dessert that should be made several hours before dinner, then put in the refrigerator to chill.

CAUTION: Never use sharp kitchen equipment or the stove or oven without asking a responsible adult to help you.

Ingredients
>   6 large oranges
>   2 bananas
>   1 cup flaked coconut
>   sugar

Directions

1. Cut oranges in half. Then scoop out sections with a small spoon into a small bowl.

2. Peel bananas and cut into ¼-inch-wide slices.

3. Put a layer of orange pieces in the bottom of a glass bowl, and sprinkle with a tablespoon of sugar. Cover with an open layer of bananas sprinkled with coconut flakes. Repeat the layers until all the ingredients are used, ending with a layer of oranges covered with coconut.

4. Cover bowl with clear food-wrap and place in the refrigerator to chill.

Central and South America and the Caribbean Islands

❖ ❖ ❖

All through this area the Christmas celebrations basically reflect the Spanish-Catholic missions, with some local customs from earlier Indian festivals. As in all Spanish-oriented countries, the twelve days after Christmas ending with Three Kings' Day is the big celebration of parties, parades, and gift giving.

In Brazil it is summer weather at Christmastime and the Christmas feast is eaten outside under a trellis, with pork roasted over a pit fire or in a very hot oven, Portuguese style. Midnight mass on Christmas Eve is often celebrated in an outside courtyard of the church or cathedral, followed by fireworks and dancing, and food stalls are set up around the square. Crèches are set up in the homes, some very elaborate.

This type of celebration is repeated all over the southern hemisphere, sometimes with masked parades on Christmas Eve and parties at friends' houses, while old Inca legends may be reenacted by their descendants. But Christmas Day is a religious day and a day of a family feast. The feasts are adapted to local foods, and the celebrations to the warm weather, though in Argentina and Chile it is true wintertime cold.

On Three Kings' Day children receive their gifts. They have filled a small box with grass for the camels who carry the Three Kings, and in the morning the grass is gone, and presents fill and overflow the box.

In the French islands of the Caribbean, French customs of Twelfth Night with its cake and gold crowns are observed; Christmas Eve supper called *rêveillon* is served, and on Christmas Eve, *Bonhomme Noël* leaves presents for the children.

The two islands Trinidad and Tobago, so close together, have slightly different ways of celebrating Christmas. In Tobago the emphasis is on cleaning and fixing up the house, with a whole week of cooking: baking hams, making sweet potato pone (mashed seasoned sweet potatoes), fruitcake, coconut ice cream, benne balls, with ham and chicken saved for Christmas lunch after church.

On Christmas Eve the house is decorated with crepe paper flowers and balloons. A branch of a large evergreen tree is brought into the house and decorated with crepe paper, cotton from a cotton tree, bells, and balloons. On that night, church groups go around singing carols, and then they feast on "pelau" chicken and rice cooked in a big pot. Church on Christmas morning is at five o'clock, then home for opening presents. Boys shoot off bamboo guns filled with carbide and fly the kites of colored paper made by their parents.

In Trinidad there is a mixture of French Creole, English, and Spanish Christmas, coinciding with the end of the Hindu harvest celebrations. Everyone joins in the varied celebrations through the long holiday, and the food is a mixture of all the home countries: mince pies, black cake (fruit cake), imported apples, potato salad, deep fried pastelles (dough-covered meat pastries), the air filled with all the smells of spices and sweet cooking.

Groups go through the street singing carols, and a Spanish group called *parang* will sing Spanish songs. Then on Christmas Eve everyone goes off to Midnight mass, and home to see what Santa brought.

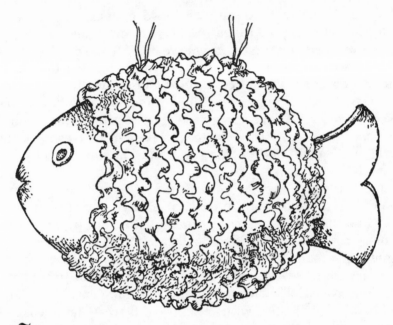

PIÑATA FISH

Beginning on December 16 in Mexico (and a few other Latin American countries), there are nine nights of a special celebration that ends on Christmas Eve. Each night after dark, groups of relatives or friends carrying lighted candles or lanterns form a small procession led by young children who each carry little figures—an angel, or Mary or Joseph. Sometimes the children are dressed as angels. This is known as the *Posada* (the Inn), and re-enacts the story of Mary and Joseph looking for a place to stay in overcrowded Bethlehem.

Knocking on the door of a relative or friend's house, the group sings the first verse of the Posada asking-for-entry song. By song from inside the house, they are refused entry. The back-and-forth request and refusal goes on until the final verse of the song when the door is opened. The group steps inside, prayers are said, then refreshments are brought out. Often there is music and dancing while the blindfolded children take turns hitting the hanging *piñata* with a long stick.

The piñatas are made of low-fired clay in the shapes of animals, birds, or fish covered all over with crepe paper ruffles. After repeated whacks with a stick the piñata will break to the delighted laughter of the children as they scramble for the candies that shower down on them.

In this project the piñata fish is made of papier-mâché formed over an inflated balloon base. The fish can be made in different sizes depending on what size balloon you buy. Remember that a papier-mâché container cannot be too large nor filled with too many candies as their weight would be too much for the papier-mâché wall to support. If you are planning for a large party, make several piñatas.

Materials and Tools

balloon, fat oval shape about 14 inches long when
   blown up
sewing thread
white household glue
papier-mâché (see last chapter)
typewriter paper
lightweight cardboard, 4 × 7½ inches
masking tape
sandpaper
facial tissues
acrylic polymer gloss medium
acrylic paint, turquoise-blue
felt-tipped pen, black
2 rolls of crepe paper streamers, 2 inches wide, azure
   blue and lavender or azure blue and nile green
assorted wrapped candies
heavy cord, see Step 11 for length
broom handle or a 1 × 36-inch wooden dowel
pencil
ruler
scissors
craft knife
flat nylon brush, 1 inch wide
round watercolor brush, #5

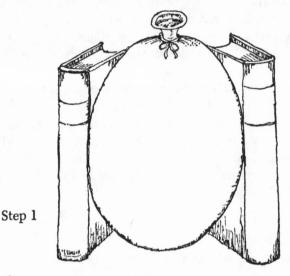

Step 1

Directions

1. Blow up the balloon until it is wide around the middle, but is still longer than it is broad. Wrap a short length of thread several times around the "neck" of the balloon and tie the ends in a knot. Brace the balloon between two books, neck upright, and fill the neck opening with household glue to prevent air from escaping from the balloon. Wait until the glue has hardened before going on to Step 3.

2. Read and follow the directions in the last chapter for making and applying papier-mâché while you are waiting for the glue to harden.

3. Cover balloon with paste-soaked strips of newspaper, crisscrossing them over the surface and building them up to the

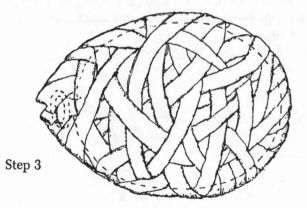

Step 3

final thickness of ½ inch. Build up the papier-mâché surface ⅛ inch at a time, drying between the layers. Bring strips to a slit point over the neck of the balloon to form the fish's open mouth. Let dry.

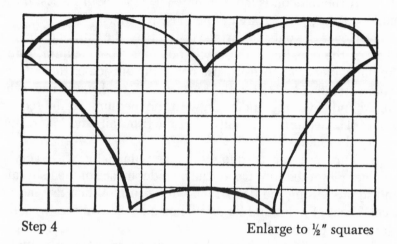

Step 4   Enlarge to ½" squares

4. Enlarge the pattern of the tail on typewriter paper by the grid method and cut out. Lay the tail pattern on the cardboard, trace around the edges, and cut out with the scissors. Hold the tail against the back of the fish and adjust the bottom curve to the curve of the fish's body. Attach the tail to the body with masking tape on both sides of the tail. Cover tail with a ⅛-inch layer of papier-mâché on each side, bringing strips over the fish's body to hold the tail in place. Gradually thicken the base of the tail to ¼ inch on each side.

5. When body and tail are completely dry, smooth the surface with sandpaper, and dust off with facial tissues. Cut a 3 ×

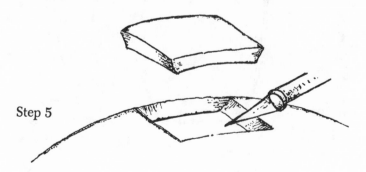

Step 5

3-inch square hole with the craft knife in the center top of the fish. Cut the sides at a sharp, inward angle so the cut-out square will not fall into the inside of the fish. The first cut will release the air from the balloon.

6. If the balloon is loose, remove it; if stuck in places to the papier-mâché, just cut away the loose parts.

7. Cover the outside surface of the fish, the tail, and the cut edges of the opening with acrylic polymer gloss medium, using the flat 1-inch-wide brush. Also cover the outside of the cut-out square and its sides. Let both areas dry. When dry, turn over the square and cover the underside with the medium. Add a second coat of the medium to the outside of the fish, tail, and square and let dry thoroughly.

8. Thin out the turquoise-blue acrylic paint with acrylic polymer gloss medium. Cover the outside surface of the fish, tail, and square, using the flat 1-inch-wide brush. When dry, add a second coat of paint and let dry. Then add the two eyes with the black felt-tipped pen.

9. The next step is to add the hanging cord to the fish piñata. The length of the two pieces of cord depends on the size of the piñata and where it is being hung. You will have to ask an adult where it can be hung, and how low it will hang, *then* measure how much cord you will need. At a third of the way from the

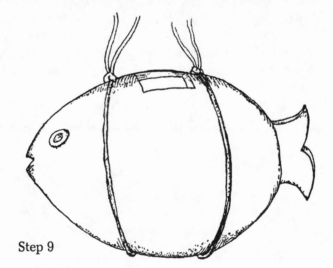

Step 9

head, bring one piece of cord around the fish, the ends held above the top, then tie a knot against the top of the fish. Repeat with the other length of cord a third of the way from the base of the tail. Bring the four ends of the cord together, centered above the fish, and tie them together into a knot.

10. The crepe paper streamers are cut into lengths that fit around the fish, ending at the center top. Each streamer will be a different length, so all will have to be fitted separately, cut, and then glued into place. Both edges of each streamer are pulled out between thumb and forefinger of each hand so the edges are ruffled. Each streamer is folded in half lengthwise, a line of glue squeezed along the outside of the fold line, and the glued area

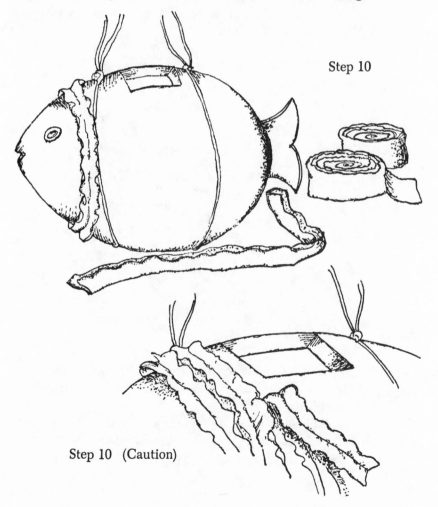

Step 10

Step 10 (Caution)

pressed against the fish. Streamers are applied close together, alternating the two colors, so the fish, except for the head and tail, is covered with ruffled crepe paper. *Caution:* leave streamer ends dangling around the edges of the 3-inch-square opening.

11. Add candy through the top opening until the fish is half full. Cover edges of opening with glue, and also cover edges of the 3-inch square with glue, then put the square in place. Cover the front and back cuts of the square with masking tape. Cover square by gluing in place the dangling ends of the crepe paper streamers, making sure that the masking tape is hidden by the streamers. Let glue dry thoroughly.

12. Hang up the piñata and you are ready for the party. Use a broom handle or a 1 × 36-inch wooden dowel to hit the piñata until the candies fall to the floor.

ANGEL OF CLAY

Christmas decorations in Mexico are often made of kiln-fired clay or papier-mâché. These flat, cookie-like shapes are painted or kiln-glazed and hung by cords over the Christmas crèche or in the windows. Angels are the most popular shape to hover over the crèche, or you can hang them on a Christmas tree or wreath.

This design is made of oven-baked or air-dried clay, decorated with acrylic paint. Before beginning the project, read the section on Clay in the last chapter. Also read the description of rolling dough in the section on Baking in the last chapter, as this will be a guide in rolling out clay—only *don't use flour on the wax paper.* Instead, moisten the paper with a little water, or use a piece of plastic cleaner's bag moistened with water.

Materials and Tools
typewriter paper
clay, oven-baked or air-dried, 2- to 5-pound box
tools for working with clay (see Clay in last chapter)
acrylic polymer gloss medium
acrylic paints, white, yellow, blue, and black
pencil
ruler
scissors
craft knife
flat nylon brush, ½ inch wide
round nylon brushes, #2 and #4
small containers for mixing paint
string

Step 2
Enlarge to ½" squares

Directions
　1. Read the section on Clay in the last chapter
　2. Enlarge pattern by the grid method on the typewriter paper, and cut out.
　3. Scoop out clay from the box and form into a ball about 3½ inches in diameter. This will be more than enough for one angel, so leftover clay can be put back in the box.
　4. Flatten the clay ball a bit and roll out with a rolling pin between slightly moistened sheets of wax paper or two pieces of slightly moistened plastic cleaner's bags. Final thickness of clay is ⅜ inch.

5. Remove top sheet of wax paper or plastic, lay the pattern on the clay, and cut around the edges with the craft knife. With a pencil point, make two holes in the clay for hanging the angel, as indicated on the pattern (page 139).

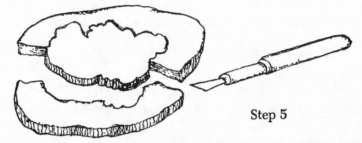

Step 5

6. Follow directions for drying in Clay in last chapter. When dry, either bake in the oven if oven-baked clay, or if air-dried clay proceed to next step. After oven-baked clay has been baked, go on to Step 7. In both cases the angel will shrink during drying.

7. Cover angel—front, back, and sides—with a coat of acrylic polymer gloss medium, using the flat brush. When dry, add a second coat and let dry (see Painting in last chapter for directions for this and Steps 8 and 9).

8. Cover face and wings with white acrylic paint mixed with a little gloss medium, using the round #4 brush, letting clay show through between the sections of wing and shoulder. Let dry, then add a second coat if needed. Cover the dress with light-blue acrylic paint, made by mixing a little of the blue paint with the white, plus gloss medium to thin it. Use the round #4 brush, brushing the length of the dress and leaving a few vertical streaks of clay showing through the paint. Let dry and add a second coat. Let dry. Mix yellow paint with a little gloss medium and paint the halo, horn, and hair. Let dry and add a second coat if needed, letting that dry. Clay is left unpainted between halo and top of head.

9. When all the paint is thoroughly dry, add the features of the face and chin line with black paint, using the #2 brush. Let dry.

10. Put a length of string through the holes to make a hanging loop (your choice of length), and tie the two ends.

Variation: Try other shapes of your own design.

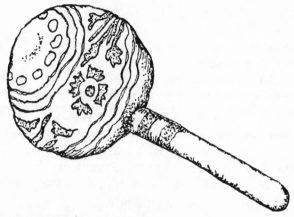

GOURD NOISEMAKER

In Central America and South America the main celebration is on January 6, the Day of the Kings (*Día de los Reyes*), as Christmas is a religious day. There are firecrackers, whistles and noisemakers, parades of people in costumes, bands and dancing, and finally the Three Kings.

This project is the small gourd noisemaker carried by children in the parade, or running through the square shaking their gourds in time to the music of the bands.

Materials and Tools
small dried gourd, 2½ to 3½ inches in diameter
wooden dowel, ⅜ inch diameter, see Step 3 for length
small stones or gravel
wood glue
enamel, ¾- to 1-ounce craft bottles, black, magenta
    red, green, and white
pencil
ruler
hand drill and ¼-inch bit
craft knife
craft saw
flat watercolor brush, ¾ inch wide
round watercolor brushes, #2 and #4

Directions

1. The Central and South American round gourds are smooth-surfaced, but you can use any small dried gourd sold in the markets even if the surface is bumpy or the gourd is slightly flattened top and bottom.

2. Drill a ¼-inch hole in the bottom of the gourd, using the hand drill. Do not lose any of the seeds inside. If there are not enough seeds to make a good rattling noise, then add a few small stones or gravel to the gourd.

3. Cut a length of dowel, using the craft saw. Measure the diameter of the gourd from top to bottom and then add 4½ inches for the handle. With the craft knife, trim the gourd end of the dowel to ¼ inch in diameter. Add wood glue to the ¼-inch top surface of the dowel, and around the bottom of the ¼-inch diameter part of the dowel. Also add glue to the edge of the drilled hole in the gourd. Put dowel into gourd and add extra glue around the joining of dowel and gourd. Using two jars or cans, brace the gourd on its top with the dowel upright, and let dry thoroughly.

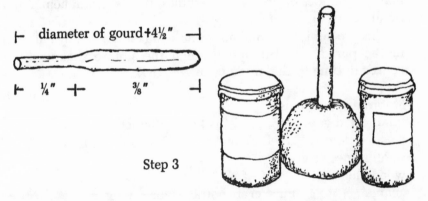

Step 3

4. Lightly paint the surface of the gourd with black enamel, using the flat brush. Let dry, then add a second coat and let dry.

5. With the #2 brush, add three irregularly-curved white lines one-third of the way from the top, and three more one-third of the way from the bottom. Make dots around the circle above the top line of white. Let dry. With the #4 brush, add magenta-red flowers and green leaves around the middle of the gourd between the white lines. See the drawing which shows a suggested contin-

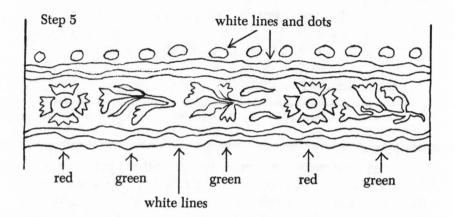

Step 5

white lines and dots

red   green   green   red   green

white lines

uous pattern of lines, flowers, and leaves. Also add a band of magenta-red and one of green around the top of the dowel handle just under the gourd. Let enamel dry, and your noisemaker is done.

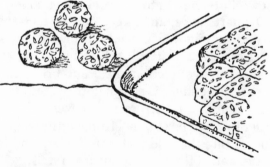

BENNE BALLS

These are round candies of sesame seeds and caramel, and are a favorite candy in Trinidad and Tobago at Christmastime. Some are made very hard, others chewy, but all are full of sesame seeds.

CAUTION: Never use sharp kitchen equipment or the stove or oven without asking a responsible adult to help you.

Ingredients
- 6 to 8 tablespoons sesame seeds, toasted
- ¾ cup half-and-half
- 5 tablespoons + 1 teaspoon corn syrup (either light or dark)
- ½ cup light brown sugar
- 1 teaspoon vanilla

Directions

1. To toast the sesame seeds, put them in a single layer in a small frying pan. Put a cover on the pan as the seeds will jump as they are heated. Place pan on the stove over a low heat. Watch the pan very carefully so the seeds will not burn, taking it off the heat, removing cover, and stirring the seeds with a spoon. The seeds brown very quickly so when they are a deep tan take them off the heat and pour them into a small bowl.

2. With a piece of paper towel, spread a thin coat of cooking oil over the inside of an 8 × 8-inch pan. Set pan aside on the working surface along with a sheet of wax paper. Put a cup of cold water, a teaspoon, and a pastry brush on the side of the stove, so they will be handy to the cooking caramel.

3. In a 1-quart saucepan, put ¼ cup of half-and-half, the corn syrup, and the sugar. Mix well with a wooden spoon until the sugar is as dissolved as it will get without heat added.

4. Put saucepan over medium heat and bring the liquid to a boil, stirring until the sugar is completely melted. Cover and let boil slowly for 3 minutes, then remove cover.

5. In order to keep the caramel from getting sugary, now dip the pastry brush into the cold water in the cup and brush down the sides of the pot, softening any sugar crystals.

6. While syrup boils, stir it very slowly in one direction, not touching the sides of the saucepan.

7. Test the syrup by taking the saucepan off the heat and dropping 3 or 4 drops of caramel from the spoon into the cup of cold water. When the soft-ball stage is reached (the drops can just be gathered together with finger and thumb), add ¼ cup of half-and-half and put saucepan back on the stove. When soft-ball stage is reached again, add the last ¼ cup of half-and-half.

Boil slowly until the firm-ball stage is reached (the syrup can be formed into a real ball).

8. Take syrup off the heat and add the vanilla and sesame seeds, stirring well, then pour and smooth into the pan. The syrup may not fill the pan completely as it should be ½ to ¾ inch deep.

9. With a knife point, make shallow crossing lines to mark off the candy into ¾-inch squares. When cool enough to touch, cut the squares apart, oil the palms of your hands lightly with cooking oil, and roll each square into a ball between your palms. Put each ball on the sheet of wax paper to cool.

10. When benne balls are cool, wrap each one in a piece of wax paper or clear plastic-wrap. Store in a covered metal box in a cool place.

Before You Begin

❖❖❖

Described in this chapter are all the craft processes you will need throughout this book. Refer to these sections whenever you start a project. You'll often have materials left over, as some products are sold in standard packages or lengths which are more than you will use for one project. Many of the projects use the same materials, so be sure to save all leftover dowels and pieces of wood, cloth and polyester fiber filling, yarn, paints, and any other scraps. Keep a scrap box so you will always know where you can find all the pieces. Also, if you have supplies left over from one project, look in the index at the end of this book for other projects using the same supplies.

Helpful Hints

Keep a bowl of water, a sponge, and paper towels beside you to clean up your hands or work surface. Also, have a box of facial tissues nearby for blotting up extra white glue or contact cement and for smoothing down just-glued paper or fabric, or wiping a paintbrush.

Put a layer of newspapers over the working surface; add another layer when the paper gets paint-spattered or sticky with glue or contact cement.

Always have a roll of self-sticking tape or masking tape handy to hold a project in place quickly.

Where to Buy Supplies

Many of the supplies needed for the projects are found in your home, in the kitchen, desk, sewing cabinet, or family workshop.

Check around the house, and ask permission to use tools or supplies before buying anything new.

Craft supplies listed in this book can be bought from an art store, hobby shop, or model-making shop. These supplies include clay, acrylic paints and acrylic polymer mediums, paper, brushes, ink, balsa wood, and all sorts of other supplies, including art and craft tools.

Hardware or paint stores are good places to buy shellac and enamel paint. Some stores carry wood dowels and small strips of balsa or other lightweight wood. Many of these supplies are sold at the lumberyard or wood shop.

Fabrics are found in fabric shops or department stores, where you can also buy beads, sequins, and buttons. Many variety stores and trimming shops also carry these supplies.

You will find that most supplies are sold only in standard quantities. However, these supplies are used in several projects. For instance, oven-baked clay is sold in 2- to 5-pound boxes depending on the manufacturer, but a box of clay is enough to make several clay projects. Tools, too, are used for many different projects.

If you do not know where the local stores are, look in the Yellow Pages of the telephone directory under Craft Supplies; Hobby and Model Construction Supplies; Artist's Materials and Supplies; Fabric Shops; Notions—Retail; Lumber—Retail; Paint —Retail; Hardware.

All craft people have to buy some of their supplies by mail order, as local stores often do not carry the exact product that is needed for a project, so send for catalogs of the firms listed below.

American Handicrafts
3 Tandy Center
Fort Worth, TX 76102

Grey Owl
Indian Craft Co., Inc.
113-15 Springfield Blvd.
P.O. Box 507
Queens Village, NY 11429

Dick Blick
Box 1267
Galesburg, IL 61401

X-acto, Inc.
48-41 Van Dam St.
Long Island City, NY 11101

BAKING AND COOKING

Some of the baking and cooking projects can be a shared pre-Christmas experience with a friend or several friends or an adult. This is always fun to do, just like being a pastry chef in a professional kitchen. Someone chops the nuts and citron, someone sifts all the dry ingredients or creams the butter and sugar together, someone rolls the dough, while everyone joins in cutting out the cookies or brushing them with egg before baking or icing them after baking. This is true with the making of casseroles or other main course recipes. Or you can try a recipe all by yourself. And, of course, cleaning up is shared by all who cooked! Then you have goodies to eat, to share with friends during Christmastime, and to take to school.

Like any other craft, baking and cooking have their own names for processes and tools, and these are explained in the following paragraphs. Baking and cooking recipes are carefully balanced to produce the final good-to-eat food. Follow a recipe *exactly* the first time you use it, then you can make minor changes to suit your own taste—more or less spices or sugar, changing the cooking time, and such like.

Do's and Don'ts

Always ask permission of an adult before using the kitchen, baking supplies, and stove. Special supplies may have to be bought at the store, so discuss the recipe with an adult who does the buying. There are some processes that will need an adult's help if you are a beginning cook, so be ready to holler, "Help!" This is especially true in using sharp knives, lighting an oven, or turning on the stove burners.

Wash hands with soap and water before beginning any cooking or baking, and wash them in between if needed.

Wear an apron or smock while cooking or baking.

Gather all ingredients and baking or cooking utensils before beginning a recipe.

Have two or more potholders or oven mitts nearby to protect your hands when taking a pan out of the oven or a pot off the stove.

Browning Nuts

Place slivered almonds on a baking sheet in a 200° F. oven. Look at them every 2 or 3 minutes so they will not burn. Pull pan forward, using a pot holder, and turn nuts over with a long-handled spoon. Take out of the oven when nuts are tan in color. Pour into a small bowl to cool.

Brushing With Egg

The tops of many cookies, cakes, or pies are brushed with beaten egg yolk or whole egg, mixed with ½ to 1 teaspoon of water, before baking so the tops will be shiny and brown. Use a table fork to beat the egg and water together. If a pastry brush or pastry feather is available, use one or the other. Or fold a piece of wax paper into several thicknesses to a strip measuring 1 × 2 inches. Dip one end into the egg and lightly "brush" over the surface of the dough.

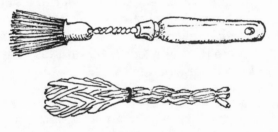

Pastry Brush and Feather

Chopping Nuts

This is a slow process, but then, cookies or cakes with nuts in them taste so good. If you are using almonds, buy slivered almonds (already sliced into narrow "sticks") as they only need to be cut in three pieces each. Work on a cutting board, and work slowly so the nuts will not jump all over the place. Also, the adult helping you may have a small chopping bowl and chopper, or a covered container with a chopper inside. Nuts can be spun in a processor but have to be watched as they turn into fine ground nuts, almost like flour, in a few seconds.

Creaming Butter or Margarine and Sugar

When collecting all the ingredients for a recipe, first take the butter or margarine from the refrigerator and measure according to the recipe. The foil covering of a stick of butter or margarine is marked off into tablespoons. Cut butter into small pieces and put into a mixing bowl. Let it stay at room temperature to soften while you gather the rest of the supplies.

When ready to start the recipe, smooth the butter or margarine with the back of a metal or wooden tablespoon until it is soft and blended together. Slowly add the sugar, pausing occasionally to smooth and blend the sugar into the butter or margarine, until all the sugar has been added. Beat a few minutes until the mixture is light and fluffy.

Dusting Citron or Other Dried Fruits With Flour

When citron is cut up in small pieces with a knife, it will all stick together in a mass, making it hard to mix into the dough. Put citron on a plate. Put a teaspoon of flour in a sieve or flour sifter and dust citron with the flour, turning the pieces over gently with a table fork until they are all separated and coated with the flour. Add more flour as needed. Raisins, too, can be dusted with flour to keep them separated.

Greasing Baking Pans

Baking pans are "greased" with either unsalted butter, margarine, or white vegetable shortening (salt will make dough stick to the pan). Take a small piece of wax paper or clear food-wrap and scoop up a little of the "grease" on the paper; rub a *thin* coat over the whole inside of the pan, adding more grease as needed. Check pan to be sure that there are no ungreased areas.

Measuring Molasses or Honey

Rub corn oil or other unflavored cooking oil over the inside surface of the measuring spoon or cup before measuring molasses, honey, or corn syrup. This will prevent these liquids from sticking to the spoon or cup.

Measuring Spoons and Measuring Cup

The spoons are a cluster of four circular metal measures: 1 tablespoon, 1 teaspoon, ½ teaspoon, and ¼ teaspoon. Cups are made of either glass, metal, or plastic, and are usually of 1-cup capacity marked off into ¼, ⅓, ½, ⅔, ¾, and 1-cup levels. Always use measuring spoons or cups, as table teaspoons or tablespoons and coffee or teacups are not standardized sizes, and recipes are based on the standard-size amounts.

Pans

Round baking pan measurements are by diameter of the pan: 7-inch, 8-inch, 10-inch, etc. Loaf pans are measured by width, length, and depth, such as 3¾ × 7¼ × 2 measured from the inside of the pan; the same applies to square or oblong pans. Baking sheets are large flat pans with shallow sides ½ to ¾ inch high, in several sizes such as 11 × 17 inches, or smaller.

Saucepans and casserole dishes are measured by their quart capacity: 1 quart, 2 quarts, etc. You can check the size by filling and refilling a measuring cup with water and pouring it into the saucepan or casserole dish, as 4 cups of liquid equals 1 quart.

Rolling Dough

Spread a sheet of wax paper long enough to cover the top of the wooden pastry board, or spread an 18-inch length on the kitchen table. Dust the surface with flour from a sieve or flour sifter. Cover with a second sheet of wax paper the same size and rub your hand over the top of the paper to transfer some of the flour to the second sheet. Remove second sheet and place it flat on the working surface, flour side up.

Form dough into a ball and put it in the center of the first sheet of wax paper. Flatten the ball with the hands and smooth sides so they are not split. Place the second sheet of wax paper on top of the dough, flour side against the dough.

With the roller, slowly flatten the dough to the thickness given in the recipe. Roll dough "around the clock" starting each time from the center and going almost to the edge. Do not try to thin out the dough in one rolling, but using medium pressure, go over and over the circle as it widens. When cracks develop along the edge, peel off the top sheet carefully and press the cracks together with a finger moistened with a little water, dusting surface of dough lightly with flour if it is sticky. Try not to wrinkle the wax paper when rolling, as this will crinkle the surface of the dough.

On the last roll or two around the circle, roll over the edge to bring it down to the same thickness as the rest of the dough. Measure the edge with a ruler to check thickness; if it is right according to the recipe, remove the top sheet of paper. Follow directions in the recipe for final cutting of dough.

Sifting Flour

Measure flour into a measuring cup. Place flour sifter on a small plate and pour flour into it. Follow recipe for any added ingredients, stirring them lightly into the flour with a spoon or table fork. Sift flour by turning the handle; add the flour left on the plate to the dough.

Starting Oven

Start the oven when you begin a baking project. Check with an adult about turning on the oven and setting it to the temperature listed in the recipe. If shelves have to be moved, do this before the oven is heated, as they are hard to handle once they are hot, and you might burn yourself.

BLOCK PRINTING WITH STYROFOAM

Styrofoam block printing designs can be cut and printed as flat solid-color designs or outline designs to be printed on colored paper. The raised design can be used over and over; it can be printed in more than one color and at any angle. Use styrofoam sheet bought at any art store, or a piece of packing material.

Materials and Tools
clear plastic wrap, 6 inches square
ball of absorbent cotton, 1¼ inches in diameter
string
masking tape
craft knife
flat plastic coffee can cover
plastic spoon
lots of newspapers

Cutting Out the Styrofoam Block

Lay your paper pattern on the block's top surface and trace around the edges of the design. With the craft knife, cut into the styrofoam along the line to a depth of ¼ inch. Then cut away the rest of the styrofoam around the outside of the design to a depth of ¼ inch. The design will then be higher than the background.

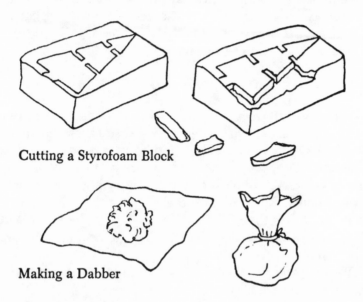

Cutting a Styrofoam Block

Making a Dabber

Making a Paint Dabber

Paint is transferred to the styrofoam block design with a dabber. To make the dabber, lightly roll a piece of absorbent cotton into a ball, 1¼ inches in diameter. Put the ball in the middle of a 6-inch square piece of clear plastic-wrap. Bring the sides of the wrap up around the cotton and tie with string close to the top of the cotton ball. Pound the dabber lightly against a flat surface to flatten the bottom.

Mixing Paint

You have a choice of paints for printing, depending on which kind is easiest for you to buy. One is acrylic paint and the other is water-base block printing ink. Both are sold in tubes and come in a number of colors.

First spread newspaper over the working surface. Squeeze out about 2 inches of paint or ink in the center of a plastic coffee can cover. Mix in a little water, stirring with a plastic spoon. The paint or ink should be quite thick.

Dip the dabber into the paint with a quick up-and-down motion; then transfer the paint to the styrofoam design with the same dabbing motion. Turn over the styrofoam block and press the raised design against a test sheet of paper. Repeat two or three times. If the paint is too thin, add more paint; if too thick, add more water and test again.

CLAY

The clay crafts described in this book are made from two special types of clay, one called *oven-baked*, the other *air-dried*. Both types are sold in 2-to 5-pound boxes depending on the manufacturer. They look, feel, and can be formed just like regular *kiln-baked* clay, which is baked at a very high temperature for several hours. For oven-baked clay, use the kitchen oven set at 250° F. for less than 2 hours, depending on the manufacturer's directions. Air-dried clay does not have to be put in the oven for hardening.

The clay objects will not be as strong as those baked at the high temperatures of a kiln.

Materials and Tools
clay of your choice
plastic dry cleaner's bag, 24 × 30 inches
small bowl for water
piece of cellulose sponge, ¾ × 3 × 3 inches
paper towels
kitchen paring knife
skewer or thin nail
small spoon
plastic bags
small mixing containers
medium sandpaper
metal cookie sheet   ⎫
separate oven thermometer   ⎬ for oven-dried clay
oven mitts or padded pot holders ⎭

Forming Clay

When you begin a project, take out a little more clay from the box than you will need. It is better to work with too much clay than too little. The unused clay can be placed in a plastic bag, closed with a plastic tie, and then put back into the box to be used for another project. You'll be able to make several projects from a box of clay.

Lay the plastic cleaner's bag over the working surface and slightly moisten the surface. Place a bowl of water and the sponge to one side of the plastic to be used to moisten the clay as you roll it. Do not use too much water, or you'll have a mud pie. And have plenty of paper towels handy to wipe your hands.

Take a piece of clay and roll it from the center outward, with a slow, even pressure of the palms of your hands. If the surface shows any cracks, run a moistened sponge over the surface, then continue to roll until you have a "sausage" shape the length and diameter you need. If you are making several rolls, put each one in a plastic bag as it is finished, and fasten the top of the bag so all pieces will stay equally moist. This is important if one part is to be attached to another part. A moist piece of clay will not *permanently* become part of a semidry piece. It will drop off when baked.

If you are sculpting a piece, keep the surface moist as you add more clay. If you have to leave the piece, even for an hour, put the piece and the rest of the clay in a plastic bag, and tie the top to keep the moisture inside. A kitchen paring knife, nail, and skewer are good tools for carving clay.

Attaching Clay Pieces to Each Other

To put pieces of a project together, use *slip* to attach them to each other.

Slip is made by mixing water and clay in a small bowl, until it is as thick as molasses. This mixture is dabbed and smoothed on the clay surface where a piece is to be added. Also put slip on the joining surface of the piece or pieces to be added. Press the two pieces together, and let dry a bit; then smooth the joint with slip until any joining cracks disappear.

Drying Clay

Let the clay project dry until it is stiff. The clay should still be slightly moist, not powdery and hard; this stage is called *leather-*

hard. Go over the surface with a dampened sponge to smooth out any cracks or rough places. If your piece is going to be covered by clothes as in the *santon,* make a few holes into the interior of the piece with a skewer or thin nail, so the interior will dry. If the project is a sculptured piece, hollow out the center to help in the drying.

When the clay object is totally dry, in two or three days, smooth the surface with sandpaper. Work carefully, as the object will be very brittle at this stage.

Oven-baked clay is now ready for baking in the oven. Air-dried clay is ready to be decorated according to the directions in the project.

Baking Clay

Put the clay object on a clean baking pan or cookie sheet. Place a baking thermometer beside it, so you can watch the temperature. Put the pan, object, and thermometer in the middle of the kitchen oven. Turn on the heat to low (150° F.), but leave the door open; let the object have a slow drying for 30 minutes. Now follow the manufacturer's directions as to final heat, and how long the object should bake. Then when done, turn off the heat, open the door, and let the object cool down in the oven.

If you do not follow this slow drying and baking process, the clay object may crack or shatter into small pieces. Any extra moisture left in the clay will expand into steam and break through the dry outside surface.

Now you are ready to decorate your clay object following directions in the project.

COOKING; SEE BAKING AND COOKING

GLUING AND CEMENTING

White Household Glue

This is used mostly on paper or fabric. Thin out the glue with a little water, so it can be brushed on with a soft ¾-inch flat watercolor brush. Put the glue on the paper in a thin coat. It is best to put glue on both facing pieces of cardboard or illustration board for a stronger bond, as they will absorb the glue

Contact Cement

To simplify the materials needed in this book, contact cement has been used in many of the projects. It makes a sure, firm bond for all materials. There are two products sold in tubes that can be bought in variety or hardware stores—Elmer's Cabinet Maker's Contact Cement and Scotch Contact Cement.

Cover both surfaces that are to be cemented together with an even white coat of contact cement, using a ½-inch or ¾-inch flat nylon brush. Let dry until shiny-clear, approximately twenty minutes. If the surface is dull, then add another coat, as too much of the cement has been absorbed. Press surfaces together carefully *as they cannot be pulled apart once the cemented surfaces are in contact.* Smooth surface with hands, or if thick wood, use a rubber mallet. You have up to two hours to put surfaces together.

GRID METHOD OF ENLARGING
AND REDUCING DESIGNS

The patterns for each project are drawn to scale on a grid. The enlarging information is printed just below the lower right-hand corner of the grid. Increase the size of the grid squares to the measurement shown—¼ inch, ½ inch, ¾ inch, or 1 inch or more.

On typewriter paper, measure and draw larger squares, matching the enlarging information. Number the lines. If the enlarged drawing is larger than a sheet of typewriter paper, tape several sheets together to make one large sheet. You can also use ¼-inch squared graph paper. Count off the number of squares needed for the enlargement, and with a ruler and pencil draw the vertical and horizontal lines. For instance, for an enlargement to 1-inch squares, count off four ¼-inch squares on the graph paper and draw a heavy pencil line. Number the lines.

Now all you have to do is draw in the lines of the pattern on the larger squares, following the lines on the smaller grid. Draw across each square in the same place and cut across each grid line at the same place. When you are finished, you will have an exact enlargement of the original pattern. See example on page 158.

To reduce a drawing, make the final grid on the typewriter paper smaller than the original pattern grid.

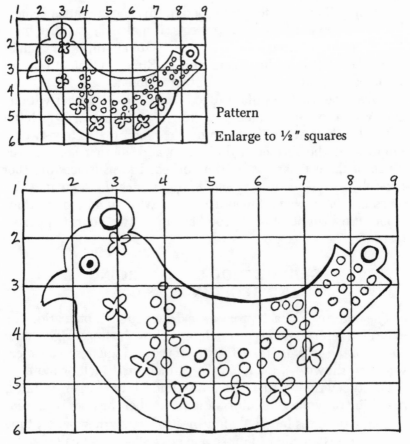

Pattern

Enlarge to ½" squares

Enlarged Drawing

LEAD-PENCIL TRANSFER PAPER

Once an enlarged pattern is made, it is easy to transfer it to the final paper, paperboard, woodboard, or fabric with lead-pencil transfer paper.

Make the transfer paper by covering a sheet of typewriter paper, or other lightweight paper, with crisscrossing strokes of a *soft* lead pencil until the surface is as dark as you can make it without digging into the paper.

To transfer a pattern, hold the final sheet of paper, board, or fabric flat on the working surface, using small pieces of tape at each corner. On top of it place the enlarged pattern drawing and hold it in place with small pieces of tape at each upper corner. Slip the transfer paper under the pattern, with the lead-pencil side downward. Draw around all lines of the pattern with a *hard* lead pencil. Lift the pattern and the transfer paper to make sure all lines have been transferred; then remove the pattern and transfer paper and continue with the project.

PAPER, CUTTING AND GLUING

Here are the basic directions for cutting all the kinds of paper, cardboard, and heavy art board you will be using in this book. The tools you will need are very simple: large and small scissors, craft knife, pencil, ruler, and eraser.

Pencil lines, whether freehand or ruled, should be drawn on the right side of any paper or cardboard unless the project directions are otherwise. The lines are a guide for scissors or craft knife, and cutting from the right side prevents tearing that side of either paper or board.

Before cutting, straight lines are always measured with the ruler and *lightly* drawn with a pencil along the edge of the ruler.

Cutting Thin Paper

Use scissors to cut thin paper: drawing paper, typewriter paper, tissue, tracing, gift wrap, shelf paper, Con-Tact or other self-sticking papers. A craft knife will sometimes tear thin paper. With the scissors, follow pencil or felt-tipped pen lines very carefully, as the finished project depends on this first outline. If you have a small design with lots of ins and outs to cut, use small scissors. Large scissors are best for long straight lines or big shapes.

Cutting Art Board or Cardboard

To begin with, put several thicknesses of newspaper under any paperboard that is to be cut with a craft knife. This will keep the flat working surface from being cut.

Most boards made of paper are too heavy to be cut cleanly with scissors. These boards include cardboard (both plain and corrugated), illustration, poster, matting, and bristol. Bristol board is thin enough to be cut with large scissors *if* the design outline is curved, but sharp straight lines should be cut with a craft knife and ruler.

A craft knife, braced straight up against the ruler's edge, is the best cutting tool for all paperboards. For clean sharp edges, always cut on the right side of the board. If you cut from the back of the board, the front surface may tear a bit, spoiling a design.

When cutting through paperboards, draw the knife lightly alongside the edge of the ruler. Repeat the cut five or six times, adding a little more pressure each time until the board is cut through to the other side. If you try to cut through the thickness of the board in one try, you run the risk of slipping off the pencil line. The pressure will be too great on the knife point, making it hard to control.

To cut a curved line with a craft knife requires patience and a steady hand. Carefully go over the line freehand many times as you slowly deepen the cut. It is better to make a few extra cuts than to have the knife slip and spoil the design.

Scoring

If your design made of paperboard needs a fold, the board is *scored* to make a sharp edge. Lay the ruler along the line on the side which will have the outward folded corner. Draw the craft

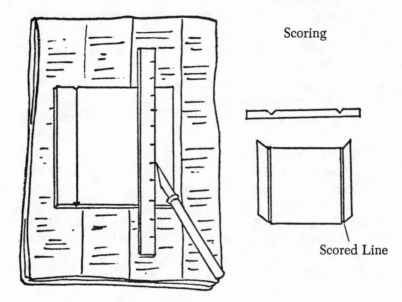

Scoring

Scored Line

knife lightly down the line, *once only*. Remove the ruler and gently ease both sides of the board away from the scored line until the correct angle is achieved.

Techniques of Gluing Paper and Board

Most of the projects in this book are held together with white household glue (such as Elmers). You will need: a small shallow plastic container to mix glue and water; a flat, ¾- to 1-inch wide watercolor brush; facial tissues; ruler; and lots of newspapers. Also have ready a small bowl of water in which to dip your fingers and brush as they get sticky, and plenty of paper towels for drying.

For most projects the glue is too thick to spread thinly and evenly over the paper or board. Squeeze glue into a small container and add a little water, drop by drop. Stir with the wooden end of the brush until it is the right thinness. Always use the flat soft brush to apply the glue to the paper.

When you are gluing a very thin piece of paper, like tissue paper, onto a heavier one, brush the glue on the heavier paper or board. If glue sinks in quickly, add a second coat; then lay the thinner piece of paper over the glue. Smooth from the center to the edges, patting lightly with a wad of facial tissues.

If the two papers are approximately the same weight, put glue on the back of the top sheet—or on both facing surfaces.

For a final smooth surface, "iron" the papers together. To do this, lay a sheet of typewriter paper over the newly glued papers. Draw the edge of a ruler firmly across the typewriter paper, from the center out to the edge. Be sure to brace the typewriter paper with your other hand at the opposite edge from the ruler's direction; this will keep the paper from slipping. Repeat the ironing motion toward the other three edges. Remove the typewriter paper and mop up any excess glue at the edges.

Ironing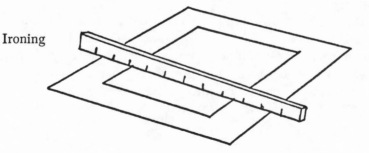

To keep glued papers from curling up while drying, put a heavy weight on top of the flat sheets; a phone book or several large books will do. Protect the surface with a clean sheet of paper. Leave the weight on until the glue is dry. This may take only a short time, or it can be a couple of hours or overnight; it all depends on how much glue was used and how dry or wet the weather is.

If you cannot use a weight on a glued section, such as the bottom of the Victorian fan decoration, hold it in place with a large paper clip or a strip of masking tape.

Cardboard and heavier art boards will need glue applied to both facing surfaces and may need more than one coat, as the glue will sink in.

Wood glue should not be thinned out. Apply it to both facing surfaces of wood, or wood and paper, with a short narrow strip of cardboard. Put a weight on top or support the glued section until dry.

When applying Con-Tact paper or any other self-sticking paper, read the manufacturer's directions carefully. If you do get bubbles under the surface, the paper can be lifted and smoothed out. Apply the paper slowly, smoothing out as you go along, patting the surface with a wad of facial tissues. The main caution is not to stretch the paper. This can be prevented by removing the backing slowly as you work, rather than taking it off all at once.

PAINTING

Acrylic Paint

The best all-around paint for the projects in this book is acrylic paint. It can be thinned with water or acrylic polymer medium for a transparent look; it can be applied thickly so as to be opaque; it is waterproof, so it can be used on all projects; and it dries quickly.

Buy acrylic paint in tubes. Use the color directly from the tube or mix two colors together to form another color. For instance, if you have one tube of blue and one of yellow, mix equal amounts together to make green. Or mix a color with white to form a lighter opaque color. To form a transparent color, mix water with the paint. The more water you add, the thinner and lighter the color will be. Always have an extra piece of the final project material handy on which to test the paint.

Before starting to mix paint, cover the working surface with several sheets of newspaper. Have extra papers handy so you can cover any spilled paint with fresh paper.

Since acrylic paint dries very quickly, use throwaway containers for mixing pans: individual aluminum foil cupcake pans are good, or small plastic drinking cups. After putting on the first coat of paint, let it dry before adding the second coat. To keep a special mixed color from drying out, put the paint in a small jar with a tight-fitting cover. This way the paint will still be liquid for the second coat.

There are two *acrylic polymer mediums* that can be used with acrylic paints. One is *gloss* which is added to the paint as a thinner, instead of water, to give the paint a high gloss when dry. The other is *matte*, which lessens the shine of the paint. Both can be used as a final coat over a painted surface, or to cover a raw wood surface before painting, so that the paint will not sink into the wood.

Always wipe off the screw top and the cap of a paint tube right after using it. Otherwise the cap will stick and be hard to take off the tube the next time you use the paint. Do the same for the jars of gloss or matte medium. And always squeeze tubes from the bottom.

When you use acrylic paint, you will need soft nylon brushes, either flat or round, as they do not leave brush marks on the paint. Always keep a jar of clean water beside you when you work. Keep the brushes in the water when you are not using them so paint will not harden on the bristles. Wipe off the water with a cloth, facial tissues, or paper towels before dipping the brush in the color. When you are through, wash the brush thoroughly with soap and water. If any paint does dry on a brush, use denatured alcohol to remove it.

Enamel Paint and Shellac

Before covering a cardboard or wood object with enamel paint, "seal" all the surfaces with one or two coats of shellac. Apply shellac with a flat watercolor brush; after using, clean the brush with denatured alcohol.

When the shellac is dry, open the can of enamel paint and stir the contents slowly and carefully with a thin stick until the surface is an even color. Flow paint on the shellacked surface with a flat watercolor brush until the surface is an even color, trying not to go over the same area too many times. After the first coat has dried, add a second coat. Let the paint dry for at least 24 hours before handling the enameled surface.

Flat paint is a nonshiny paint with an oil or latex base. Brush it on over an undercoat of shellac, the same as for enamel paint.

Warning: If the shellac coat or the first coat of enamel has a rough surface when dry, smooth it out with sandpaper before adding a second coat.

PAPIER-MÂCHÉ

Papier-mâché is not only an easy craft, it is a recycling one, as it uses newspaper as the basic material.

First, tear or cut newspapers into strips, ½ inch wide and as long as the sheet of paper. Next, mix a bowl of paste. The amount should depend on the project you are making. If it is a large one and you run out of paste, just make a second bowlful. Start with ½ cup of flour; then slowly add ¼ cup of water, stir-

½ cup flour   ¼ cup water   1 tablespoon white glue

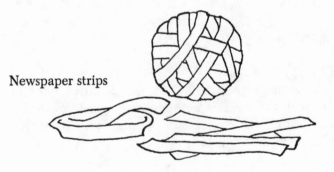

Newspaper strips

ring all the time so that the flour will not lump. When it is well mixed, add enough water to make a thin paste. Add 1 tablespoon of white glue or wood glue to the flour and water mixture and stir until well mixed.

Pour the paste into a wide, shallow dish. Pull strips of paper through the paste and wrap them around a mold. Several layers of paper are crisscrossed over each other to build up a thickness of ⅛ to ¼ inch or more, all over the mold. After you have built up the right thickness of paper, let the object dry until it is stiff enough to hold its shape.

When papier-mâché is completely dry, go over the surface with sandpaper and wipe off dust with a facial tissue. Cover surface with either shellac or acrylic polymer medium (either gloss or matte). Paint surface with enamel paint or acrylic paint that has been mixed with the medium. You can cover the acrylic paint with a final coat of the medium.

SALT DOUGH

Here is the master recipe for making a quantity of salt dough:
    2 cups flour
    1 cup salt
    1 cup cold water

Mix flour and salt together in a bowl. Slowly add one cup of water, stirring all the time. If the dough is too sticky, add a little more flour. If you are not using all the dough right away but will use the rest within a day or two, place the leftover dough in a plastic bag, seal, and put in the refrigerator.

If the project needs only a small quantity of dough, follow this formula: whatever the quantity of flour, add half that quantity of salt and water. For instance, 4 tablespoons flour, 2 tablespoons salt, 2 tablespoons water.

Squeeze and mold the dough into the shape you want, adding pieces where needed. Let dry until completely hard. Sandpaper any rough spots, then dust off surface with a facial tissue. Cover surface with acrylic polymer medium, either matte or gloss, or shellac. Let dry, then paint with acrylic paint mixed with either medium or with flat paint. A top coat of either medium or shellac can be added.

SEWING FABRIC

Sewing a Strengthened Seam

With a ruler, measure the seam width shown on the pattern with right sides of the fabric together. Pin the two thicknesses of fabric together on the seam line. Thread the needle with matching thread and make a knot at the free end.

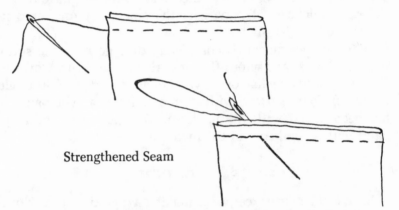

Strengthened Seam

Sew small stitches all along the seam line, removing the pins as you stitch. When you reach the end, tie off the thread with several stitches in the same place. Loop the thread through itself to make a small knot. Now strengthen the seam by sewing over the same line, but reverse the position of the running stitches. The needle and thread will go under the stitch that shows on the surface, then over the unstitched space. This will make a solid line of stitching.

Optional: If you are allowed to use the sewing machine, use it for the seams, or ask an adult to sew the seams for you.

Back-Stitch

This stitch is also used for seams and produces the same final seam as the strengthened seam. The pattern of stitching is: one stitch over the two thicknesses of cloth followed by one under the cloth; then one stitch back over the exposed cloth; then forward under the cloth for the length of two stitches; then back one stitch over the exposed cloth. Follow this pattern until the seam is complete

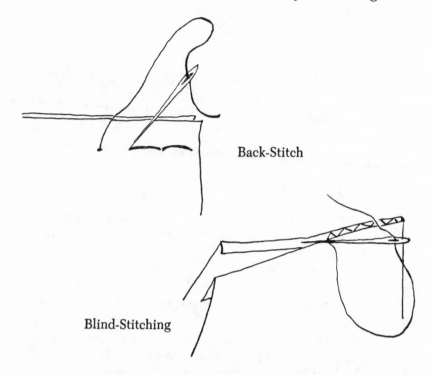

Back-Stitch

Blind-Stitching

Blind-Stitching

Blind-stitching is used to close an opening or a slit in fabric. Turn under the material on each side of the opening, holding it in place with pins. Sew the opening together by putting the needle and thread through the folded edge—first one side, then the other. Pull the sides toward each other so they just meet as you sew along the opening. Finish off the end with an over-and-under stitch, looping the thread through the last stitch. Cut off excess thread.

Gathering

To gather fabric, make tiny running stitches with needle and thread. Make two or three rows of stitches, the first row ⅛ inch from the edge of the fabric, the rest ⅛ inch apart. When you have finished a row, leave about 4 inches of thread at the end of the stitching; cut the thread and tie a knot in the end. When all the rows have been stitched, gently ease the fabric along the stitching

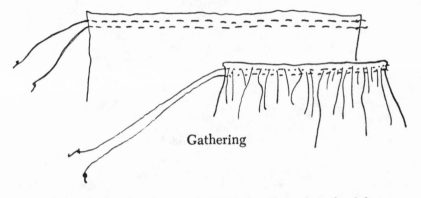

Gathering

while pulling on the extra lengths of thread. Gather the fabric as tight as you need to. Tie the threads together and cut off the excess thread.

Hemming

For narrow hems, turn the edge of the fabric twice over on itself on the wrong side and pin in position. Thread the needle and put a knot in the other end of the thread. Take small, angled stitches along the edge of the hem, taking up a bit of the base fabric and a bit of the folded edge of the hem with the needle's point. Pull the thread through and then make the next stitch. Try not to take too much of the base fabric, for the stitches will show on the right side.

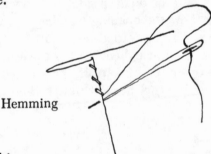

Hemming

Overhand Stitching

This is sometimes called *whipping*. The overhand stitch is used to hold two pieces of fabric together with a very narrow seam along their edges.

The edges of the two pieces of fabric are placed together, right sides facing each other. The overhand stitch goes through the

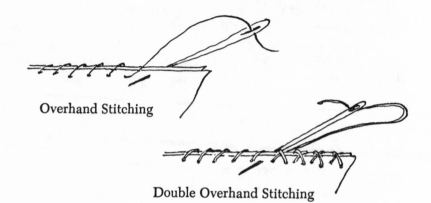

Overhand Stitching

Double Overhand Stitching

two pieces of fabric, just in from their edges, then over the top edges, then back again through the fabric. This prevents the fabric from fraying, which is very useful when working with loosely woven materials. The stitch is also used for nonfraying, heavy fabrics, such as felt or heavy plastic, to reduce a bulky seam. With these fabrics the seam is often placed on the right side of the fabric as a decorative feature.

A double overhand stitch has the same first row of the plain overhand stitch. Then, starting from the other end of the seam, make a second row of overlapping stitches. The stitches are made in-between the first row of stitches.

WORKING WITH WOOD

Balsa Wood

Balsa is a very soft, lightweight wood. It is easy to cut with a small craft saw or a sharp X-acto craft knife.

Balsa wood is sold in 36-inch-long pieces; widths vary from 3 to 6 inches, with thicknesses of ⅛, ¼, and ½ inches.

All wood has a "grain." If you are using a sharp craft knife, it

#19 blade

Craft Knife   #5 handle

will be easy to cut with the grain. When cutting across the grain, you will have to make a series of shallow cuts, repeated along the same line so that the wood will not splinter or chip. Use an X-acto #19 blade in a #5 handle. Brace the knife against a ruler so the edge of the cut will be clean and even.

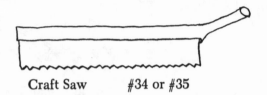

Craft Saw   #34 or #35

A clean cut can be made both with the grain and against the grain using a craft saw. The X-acto blades are #34, ¾ inch wide, and #35, 1 inch wide; both have a cutting edge 4½ inches long. They both fit into a #5 handle.

In all sawing, the cutting stroke is only one way; the return stroke of the saw does not cut into the wood. Some craft saw blades cut on the downstroke, other on the upstroke, so test the blade on scrap wood.

All cut edges have to be smoothed, first with a wood file, then with medium grade sandpaper, the dust wiped off with a cloth or facial tissue.

Dowels

Dowels are lengths of wood which are shaped into circles, triangles, squares, or rectangles. Sizes vary from ⅛ inch to 2 or 3 inches in diameter, usually 36 inches long.

Most hardwood dowels can be cut or carved with the same tools used for balsa wood. Use the craft saw to cut across the grain, which means cutting across the diameter of the dowel. The craft knife used for balsa wood is also very good for carving or whittling hardwood. If you have to whittle out a section of a thicker dowel (1 to 3 inches or more), you can make a clean saw cut around the edge and then cut out the wood to that edge.

Drilling

To make holes in wood or other materials, use a hand drill with a bit the same size as the hole you want to drill. Bits are

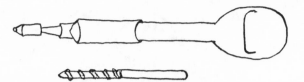

Hand Drill and Bit

metal cylinders with a cutting edge; they come in many sizes and are set into the drill whenever needed.

Finishing Wood

After the carving or whittling is done, go over the rough parts of the surface with a small wood file. Work over all areas until the surface is smooth. Then rub all surfaces with medium sandpaper until the wood is satin smooth. You may have to finish flat boards in the same way.

Finish the wood with a base coat of white shellac or acrylic polymer medium, either matte or gloss, to seal the wood surface. This will keep the paint from soaking into the wood. Always put on two coats of this base. Let the first coa dry, then sandpaper the surface lightly, dust off, and add the second coat. It is best to use a ¾ inch wide soft watercolor brush for the shellac and a nylon brush for acrylic polymer medium

Index

✦ ✦ ✦

- A -

Advent, 1, 40, 41, 102
Advent Calendar, 41–45
Acrylic paint, 23, 41, 55, 66, 75, 83, 91, 110, 133, 139, 153, 162–163
Acrylic polymer mediums, 23, 66, 75, 133, 139, 162–163
Almond paste, 32, 33, 70
Ambrosia, 128–129
Angels, 45–47, 74, 138–140

- B -

Baking and Cooking, 148–152
Balsa wood, 78, 83, 169–170
Basil, 61
Befana, 73
Bethlehem, 1, 2, 12, 72
Black Peter, 65–66
Block printing, styrofoam, 109–111, 152–154
Bonhomme Noël, 21, 131
Boxing Day, 5
Bristol board, 36, 41, 45, 49, 66
Button and carpet thread, 19, 55, 88, 104, 113

- C -

Candies, 31, 48, 66, 116–117, 133, 143–145
Candles, 40, 76, 79, 82, 83
Cardboard, 16, 36, 45, 49, 66, 133

Carols, 13–14, 40, 65, 77, 131
Chenille balls and stems, 98
Christ Child, 1, 61, 62, 72, 73
Christmas Card, 109–111
Christmas crib, 54, 109
Christmas customs, 1–3
    Brazil, 2, 130
    Caribbean Islands, 2, 131, 143
    Central and South America, 2, 130, 132–133, 138, 141
    China, 97
    England, 4–6, 8–9, 12, 13–14
    France, 21, 22–23, 30–31, 32–33, 35–36
    Germany, 40, 41, 45, 48, 51–52
    Greece, 61, 62
    Holland, 65–66, 69
    India, 2
    Italy, 13–14, 22, 72–73
    Medieval, 8–9, 14, 15
    Middle Ages, 8, 13
    Philippines, 102–103
    Puerto Rico, 2
    Scandinavia, 76–77, 79–80, 82–83, 87
    Thailand, 2, 91–96
    Trinidad-Tobago, 131, 143
    United States, 3, 108–109, 112–113, 117–118, 121, 123–124, 126
Christmas Day, 1, 2, 61, 65, 72, 73, 76, 102, 108
Christmas Eve, 1, 21, 40, 61, 102, 108, 109, 130, 132

Christmas greens, 2, 5–6, 7, 40, 82
Christmas-package seals, 41, 49
Christmas markets or fairs, 21, 23, 51–52, 73
Christmas Paper Crackers, 30–32
Christmas Star (*Parol*), 103–107
Christmas Stocking, 108, 112–115
Christmastime, 5, 13, 51
Christmas tree, 5, 16, 40, 45, 48, 77, 82
Christmas tree decorations, 2, 15–16, 18–19, 40, 45, 48, 51, 52, 77–79, 97, 108, 131, 138
Clay, 23, 73, 75, 133, 138, 139, 154–156
Cloves, whole, 12, 14, 63
Contact cement, 16, 45, 83, 91, 157
Con-Tact paper, 49
Cookies, 9–11, 48, 51–54, 61, 62–64, 69–71
Cornucopia, 19, 48–51
Courambiades, 62–64
Crayons, 41
Crèche, 22–23, 54, 73–75, 130, 138 (see Christmas Crib, Nativity Scene)
Cromwell, Oliver, 5, 8, 108

- D -

Day of the Kings, 141 (see Epiphany, Three Kings' Day, Twelfth Night)
Dowels, wood, 16, 83, 104, 133, 141, 170
Druids, 4, 5

- E -

Enamel paint, 78, 141, 163–164
Epiphany, 1, 61, 72, 73 (see Three Kings' Day, Twelfth Night)

- F -

Fabric, 16, 23, 55, 91, 113, 123, 124
Father Frost, 40, 76
Feathers, 147
Felt, 113
France, 21, 22–23, 30–31, 32–33, 35–36

- G -

Germany, 40, 41, 45, 48, 51–52, 54
Glastonbury thornbush, 4
Gluing and Cementing, 156–157
Gourd Noisemaker, 141–143
Greece, 61–62
Grid method, 157–158
Grosgrain ribbon, 16, 45

- H -

Helpful Hints, 146
Holland, 65, 69

Honey Spice Cookies, 51–54
Hot Mulled Cider, 13–14

- I -

Illustration board, 49, 83
Initial Letter Cookies, 69–71
Italy, 13–14, 22, 72–75

- J -

Julenisse, 76
Jultomten, 77

- K -

King Arthur, 14
King Henry the Eighth, 5

- L -

Lace, 19, 118
Lead pencil transfer paper, 41, 158–159
Luther, Martin, 40

- M -

Magi, 1, 2, 8, 12, 62, 72 (see Three Kings)
Marking pens, 16, 41, 45, 55, 91, 104, 110, 133
Medieval, 8–9, 14, 15
Middle Ages, 8, 13
Middle East, 2, 9
Midnight Mass, 2, 21, 73, 102, 130
Mincemeat-Filled Cookies, 8–11
Mincemeat pies, 2, 8–9
Mincemeat turnovers, 9, 11
Mistletoe Ball, 5–8
Moore, Clement Clarke, 108
Mummers, 4

- N -

Nativity Scene, 73, 102 (see *Crèche*, Christmas Crib)
Nativity Scene Figures, 73–75, 109
New England Bread Stuffing, 121–123
Nuremberg Fair, 51–52
Nuremberg *lebkuchen*, 51–54

- O -

Oranges, 12, 76, 108, 126, 127, 128, 129

- P -

Paint, enamel, 78, 141, 163–164
Paint, flat, 83
Pagan customs, 1, 4, 5–6, 21, 40, 72, 76, 87, 130

Painting, 162–164
Paper
    Bristol board, 36, 41, 45, 49, 66
    Cardboard, 16, 36, 45, 49, 66, 133
    Con-Tact, 49
    Crepe streamers, 133
    Gift wrap, 19, 31
    Gold or silver, 19, 31, 35, 36
    Gold foil, 36
    Heavy white drawing paper, 41, 110
    Illustration board, 49, 83
    Tissue, 23, 55, 104
    Wax, 117, 139, 145, 151
Paper, Cutting and Gluing, 159–162
Papier-mâché, 66, 133, 164–165
Piñata Fish, 132–138
Polyester fiber filling, 124
Pomander Ball, 6, 8, 11–13, 19
Posada, 109, 132
Proud Peacock, 97–101
Puffed Rice Molasses Balls, 116–117
Putze, 109

- Q -

Queen Elizabeth I, 5, 12
Queen Victoria, 5, 18–19

- R -

Réveillon, 21, 131
Ribbon, 6, 12, 16, 23, 31, 45, 49, 88, 113,
    118, 124
Ribbon Christmas Ball, 117–121

- S -

Saint Francis of Assisi, 13, 22, 73
Saint Lucia, 72–73, 77, 79–80
Saint Lucia Buns ("Cats"), 79–82
Saint Nicholas, Saint Nicholas Eve and Day,
    1, 61–62, 65–66, 69, 108, 112–113
Salt dough, 83, 165
Santa Claus (Klaus), 5, 40, 76, 77, 108 (see
    Saint Nicholas)
Santons of Provence, 22–30
Scandinavia 76–89
    Denmark, 76
    Finland, 76
    Norway, 76, 77–79
    Sweden, 77, 79–82, 87–89

Sewing Fabric, 166–169
Shakespeare, William, 5
Shellac, 78, 83, 163–164, 171
Sinterklass (see Saint Nicholas)
South Carolina Orange Sweet Potatoes,
    126–127
Spices, 8, 14, 52, 76
Square-Top Cornucopia, 48–51
Straw Fish, 90–96
Styrofoam block, 55, 110, 152–154
Supplies, Where to Buy, 146–147

- T -

Thailand, 2, 90
Three Kings' Day, 1, 2, 72, 73, 102, 130,
    141 (see Epiphany, Day of Kings,
    Magi, Twelfth Night)
Tinsel cord, 36, 118
Twelfth Night, 1, 5, 6, 21, 32–33, 35–36,
    40, 72, 77, 131
Twelfth Night Cake, 21, 32–35, 131
Twelfth Night Crowns, 21, 32, 33, 35–39,
    131
Twelve Days of Christmas, 2, 5, 8, 14, 21,
    130

- V -

Victorian Christmas, 9, 15, 18–19, 112
Victorian Fan Decoration, 18–20

- W -

Walnuts, 15–16
Walnut Shell Cradle, 15–18
Wheat Wreath, 87–89
White household glue, 16, 19, 23, 36, 41,
    55, 98, 104, 113, 118, 133, 156
Wire, 6, 16, 88, 98, 104
Wooden beads, 16, 45
Wooden Cutouts for the Tree, 77–79
Wood Glue, 141
Wood, Working with, 169–171
Woolly Sheep, 54–60

- Y -

Yule, 4, 77
Yule Log, 4, 21, 40